Just Walk With Me

'I commend this book to those thinking about, or engaged in youth work, especially in tough urban areas. It pulls no punches, telling of the challenges and the difficulties. This diary arises from the crucible of experience and is honest about the struggles, pitfalls and joys. The stories told here will resonate with the experience of others working on "the edge". I commend it to all who seek to engage with unchurched young people today.'

The Rt Revd David James, Bishop of Bradford

'A bitingly honest, extremely engaging and at times laugh-out-loud funny account of no holds barred youth work. If you want to have a new-found respect for what the church can accomplish in Britain then look no further. It's a cliché but every church leader *should* read this book. Today's generations simply don't speak the language most churches are trying to communicate with, we have to listen to risk-taking pioneers like e:merge if we're going to understand how to invite marginalised young people to embark on a journey of faith.'

Rachel Gardner, youth worker and leader on BBC2's Romance Academy

'*Just Walk With Me* is the most inspirational and challenging account of urban mission I have read for a long time. This is it – raw and real. There is nothing romantic here. Simply, ordinary people made extraordinary by a remarkable God and having an amazing impact. We should pray for more like Niki and Yan because these are the people that our cities are crying out for. These are the people who, in the power of God, change worlds.'

Simon Downham, Vicar, St Paul's, Hammersmith

'Gut-wrenchingly excellent. Here it is in glorious mono-chrome. No positive spin, no happy endings levered in. Just the rubber of faith hitting the pot-hole covered road of modern life in Bradford. This book won't make you happy immediately, but if that's what you want then maybe that's the problem. You'd better read this journey of long-haul discipleship.'

Andy Flanagan, singer/songwriter and worship leader for Youthwork the Partnership

'This book makes an important contribution to a difficult and demanding area of ministry – that of working with those alienated in our inner cities. At times brutally honest and uncompromising, it simply reflects the reality of working in this type of ministry. However, peppered throughout is the pure joy that shines through when Christ moves in a person's life, and their journey into faith begins. And suddenly, despite all its heartaches, it all becomes worthwhile.'

Barrie Thomas, Director, Living Well Trust, Carlisle

Just Walk With Me

A true story of inner-city youth work

Jude Simpson
and
e:merge

Authentic

MILTON KEYNES ● COLORADO SPRINGS ● HYDERABAD

First published 2008 by Authentic Media
9 Holdom Avenue, Bletchley, Milton Keynes,
Bucks, MK1 1QR, U.K.
1820 Jet Stream Drive, Colorado Springs, CO 80921, U.S.A.
OM Authentic Media, Medchal Road, Jeedimetla Village,
Secunderabad 500 055, A.P., India
www.authenticmedia.co.uk
Authentic Media is a division of IBS-STL U.K., limited by
guarantee, with its Registered Office at Kingstown Broadway,
Carlisle, Cumbria CA3 0HA.
Registered in England & Wales No. 1216232.
Registered charity 270162

British Library Cataloguing in Publication Data

A catalogue record for this book is available from the
British Library

ISBN-13: 978-1-86024-611-1

www.judesimpson.co.uk
Cover Design by fourninezero design.
Print Management by Adare Carwin
Printed and bound in Great Britain by
J.H. Haynes & Co., Sparkford

Contents

Foreword

This interesting book can be read in a number of ways.

First, it is a stark reminder, especially in the earlier chapters, of the extent and depth of poverty and disadvantage still to be found in Britain, of which 'Bradford 4' is a prime example.

Second, it challenges many of the assumptions about Christianity which at least some of the major characters in this book seem to have held once upon a time and which, they fear, others in the churches still do. In particular they come to reject the idea that God is judgemental, narrow-minded and only really interested in a negative morality and young people becoming Christians. They certainly don't believe that traditional-style 'conversions' are going to solve everything or, in the short term, anything very much at all.

But third, and most important, this book, in its modest, narrative way, nails its colours to the mast as to what really counts in youth work of this kind including: a holistic approach which is concerned about all the needs of young people – practical, emotional educational and not just 'spiritual'; cultural sensitivity;

upholding standards without breaking relationships; good professional management of projects and people; participation of stakeholders in responsible tasks; affirmation rather than criticism; and, above all perhaps, as implied by the book's title, being prepared to be there in the community and stay long enough to build trust, which for some has meant staying for all their working lives.

And it is here that theology and practice seem to meet most powerfully, where the unconditional love of a God who stays with us is modelled in the commitment of these youth workers.

This book, which deserves to be widely read and discussed, is largely made up of the diary of a youth worker during her first year in Bradford, newly-arrived from a very different background, interspersed with the reflections, born out of longer experience, of a more senior colleague. Both are stories of changing attitudes, maturing insights and some remarkable achievements (not least in preparing school drop-outs for the world of work) against a challenging background of urban deprivation, anxieties about funding and an often puzzled and insufficiently supportive institutional church. Through it all shines a measure of faith, hope and love which offers us both much to learn and a great deal of inspiration.

Michael H. Taylor, Emeritus Professor of Social Theology,
University of Birmingham and former director of
Christian Aid

Introduction

When e:merge asked me to write this book, I didn't have a clear idea of what I should say. I chatted ideas over with a couple of the key staff at e:merge and then went up to Bradford to visit the project. Whilst there, I interviewed many of the staff and met some of the young people. In doing so, I quickly saw that there was a strong and incredibly important story to tell about the challenges of living in an area of the country where hope and comfort were elusive: could the grace and generosity of God make a difference there?

The story was also about the extraordinary and often shameful gap between the realities of life for many people in deprived neighbourhoods and the church's understanding of what it constitutes to offer salvation and acceptance to all those who need it. I was personally struck by the sense that we have sometimes allowed our comfortable church situations to become stumbling blocks for people who are longing for an encounter with Jesus, but who have different expectations and experiences of life from our own.

I wrote this book on the basis of interviews with the staff and young people at e:merge, and in close consultation with them. The names of all the young people in this book have been changed. Some of the details of their stories and families have also been changed, in order to respect identity and privacy. Aside from those changes, this book is a true story, and the essential truths which are illustrated by the stories, remain intact.

As I wrote this book, the story took me over, and I found myself changed by it. I hope you will be too.

Jude Simpson

'On our journey this year, we saw many "firsts" in our work. We formed a new organisation, moved into a new building, employed new staff and delivered new activities – a lot has changed over the past year . . .

In April we employed a new outreach youth worker . . . Niki has settled in well and is making a very positive impact on the young people and the e:merge team. We are excited about the possibilities that Niki will develop over the coming years, including a youth council and facilitating the process of two young people becoming directors with e:merge.'

e:merge Annual Report 2005

1

Just For a Year

Yan

Niki came for an interview and she was great. Very professional. Very lively. She gave a great presentation and had experience of youth work, but she wasn't at all sure whether or not she should take the job. Her experience was from a very different environment from Bradford 4. She was from Macclesfield and had worked there and in Devon. She was a nice girl – trendy-looking, with oblong glasses and light, blonde hair. She was polite and well brought-up. If you wanted someone to run a youth club for high-achieving pupils in a posh school, then Niki could have done it with her eyes closed. But Bradford?

Diarmuid phoned her and offered her the job, but she just said, 'I'm not sure.' He persuaded her to come up again for a couple of days to have a look round. That often works when people are uncertain. She came back and met some more of the staff, spent some time with the young people and she was hooked. She made a decision to take the job.

My earliest impression of Niki was that she was a very 'Christiany' Christian. A stereotypical evangelical, full of, 'Ooh, Jesus is good, I'm so happy, the world is such a great place!' That was Niki in the beginning in my experience, and that's where I've been in the past as well. In my own journey of faith, over the years, I've been at various points, and at one point, I was a similar, 'Jesus is good and nothing is bad, everything can be fixed with a nice, quick prayer,' sort of Christian. So I could recognise some of that in her. And because I know how this area of Bradford has worked on me since I've been here, and how it has challenged me and changed me, I looked at Niki and thought to myself, 'Oh yeah, there's a nice journey ahead for you!'

So I prayed that she had strong guts as well as good looks, because otherwise she wouldn't be able to stick it. And then we'd have to start recruiting all over again.

Niki's diary, 30 March 2005

When they offered me the job, I didn't want it. I went to the interview, and came away thinking, 'This looks really tough. If they offer it to me, I'll say "no".' Then Diarmuid rang – he's the manager of the project, sort of runs it all – and he offered me the job. I was completely unsure, but he said, 'Look, why don't you just come back and have a look round for a day or two to see what you think?' There was no reason not to do that – I could still say no. So I went, last week.

The project is called 'e:merge'. It's based in this big, dark church building in the middle of a sort of estate area in South East Bradford – they refer to it as 'BD4' because that's the postcode.

The surrounding streets are part housing and part industrial, and there are big main roads on three sides. It's pretty bleak. The building is clean inside, though, and well looked after. There's an area with a pool table and some sofas, a tuck shop for the kids, a few computers they can use for job searching and a little kitchen with a hatch. Then there's a sort of big folding screen along one side that has been decorated with pictures, cartoons, Bible verses and quotes from famous people. Right across one side of it, it says, 'Don't let anyone look down on you because you are young' (from 1 Tim 4:12), which I liked. Beyond the screen is the main body of the church, under the steeple, which they use for larger gatherings and 'Xstream', which is their Friday night youth church. It's a big empty space with stone pillars. The offices and a couple of classrooms open off the main area. These are quite dingy and basic – though everyone has their own desk and computer and a proper adjustable chair.

I met Yan and Sharon again. They are the married couple in charge of all the youth work – they interviewed me the first time I came up. They seem nice. Yan's from South Africa and used to be a policeman. You can kind of see why. He's big and burly, and I can't imagine he ever minces his words. Sharon is gentler, but equally determined. Then there's John, who runs the Academy, which is their youth training programme. He used to be a professional footballer. Then there's Sarah, who is the office administrator. She's a Bradfordian and is very loud.

I saw some of the young people at the drop in – teenage boys with their trousers half way down their bums, and girls with trainers, big gold hoop earrings and hair flopping over their eyes. I didn't really chat to them much or anything, and none of them said hello or asked me any questions, but you can see the need. They were queuing up to come in, waiting for drop in to start. They kept ringing the bell, over and over, and Sarah in the office would get on the intercom and yell, 'IT'S STILL 2 MINUTES TO 3, I'VE TOLD YOU, YOU CAN'T COME IN YET!'

It's all quite harsh and I didn't fancy it to be honest, but something stopped me saying no straight away.

I got home and I didn't really want to do it, so I've spent the last 3 days trying to get God to tell me I <u>have</u> to do it. To go somewhere that tough, I decided I needed God to make it really, specifically clear to me. But he didn't.

And then somehow, I thought it would be good to do it just for a year. I still don't know quite how I came to that decision. I've just rung Diarmuid and told him I'll take the job. I keep saying to myself, if I don't like it, I don't have to stay any longer than a year. Not that I said that to him – I just said, 'Yes, I'll do it.' So I'm going to start on 11 April.

What have I let myself in for?

2

Break Rules, Not Trust

Yan

Some years ago, we had a gang of kids that hung round the community centre causing trouble. This would be back in 2000 when we'd only just recruited John, our first permanent staff member. Absolute nightmare kids they were. They did it all – breaking into our cars, puncturing our tyres by sticking nails in them. They smashed the community centre window at one point, and because there was a fridge the other side of the window, they just pushed the fridge over, and caused damage to all the electrics and stuff. It was totally random what they did. We decided we needed to get a security camera put up, but the guy who came to put it up couldn't, because they kept throwing stones at him as he was up on his ladder. As soon as he put his foot on the ladder, they would just get these stones and pelt him.

It was stupid, mindless stuff. There used to be a bus that stopped in front of the community centre, but they started pulling the plug on the bus. Every time a bus stopped outside they would break open the flap at the back and literally pull the plug on it so that it stopped. And the bus driver would get out and walk round to the back of the bus, with them just watching, and he'd plug it back in, and close the flap, and walk back round to the front of the bus, get in, sit down, and as soon as he did that, they'd do it again – they'd lift up the flap and unplug the bus. And the poor bus driver, all he could do was get out, go round the back and plug it in again. It was ridiculous. You'd see buses outside for literally twenty to twenty-five minutes because they just couldn't go anywhere. In the end, they started re-routing buses so they didn't come down our road any more it was that bad. It was absolutely ridiculous.

Sometimes you'd walk out of the community centre and there'd be stones raining down on you. You'd look up and these lads were chucking stones at you. It was mostly small stones and pebbles, but they did it to the dustbin men, too, and it would sometimes be bricks and stuff – the kind of thing that could actually kill someone.

This carnage just went on and on – there was no end to it. John's car was broken into twenty-six times that year – every two weeks – and windows were smashed at the centre. It was constant. We were getting phone calls threatening to beat us up. The families of some of the staff were too afraid to come and visit them.

The kids who were doing all this stuff knew they were untouchable. They were under sixteen at the time, so we'd call the police and when the police got there, the kids would just swear at them and walk away. The police themselves knew it was pointless doing anything, because if they did arrest them and take them in, they'd all simply say, 'No comment' to all their questions, and waste a lot of their time. They knew from the older kids around exactly what to do if they were interviewed. You think, well, if the police are powerless, what can we do? We were tearing our hair out. Every day there was an incident. We decided at one point to keep a record of the incidents, so we got a book and we started a list, but the list just got longer and longer. All we could do was know exactly which incidents had happened when, because we had a nice long list of them, but that didn't help stop the incidents happening!

In the end, we had this idea. What we decided to do was, every time we saw these young people we would preach at them. Whenever we saw one of them, or a group of them in the street, we started going straight up to them and preaching – talking really 'Christian' to them, walking up and saying, 'You know lads, Jesus loves you; he really loves you; he died on the cross for you.' Once we started, we got quite into it. We'd just say whatever bizarre stuff came into our heads, thinking on the spot, like, 'See that baseball cap you're wearing on your head, well that's like God – it protects you from the rain, and God wants to protect you because he loves you, and he fits you, just like a baseball cap. Except God's not back to front – no – he's a God of order.' A lot of it felt totally random. We weren't consciously trying to convert the lads – there was no sense of that whatsoever – but simply defending ourselves by preaching. We preached so consistently that it got to the point where they'd start walking away as soon as they saw us, and we'd have to raise our voices to preach at them across the street, just because they hated it so much, and it would move them on, and we'd have a few moments of peace.

There was one time I looked out of the window of the Vine – the building we were in back then – and I saw a group of about ten of these young lads crossing the road. They were running and looking behind them in a terrified sort of way, and I thought to myself, 'Oh no, what's going on there? Some kind of trouble'. The next minute, though, I saw John come into view. He was preaching at them – just running after them, waving his arms and preaching. And all I could see was these guys, who had been so tough and trying to get us in every way possible, completely scarpering from John's preaching! It was hilarious. I'm not sure it was classic youth work practice, but in those particular circumstances, for what we needed right then, it worked.

Niki's diary, 19 April 2005

Yesterday, and today in the evening, I did detached work with Yan for the first time. The idea of detached work here is the same as I've done before – going round the area, talking to the young people we meet on the streets, introducing ourselves and inviting them to the drop in sessions at e:merge. There are loads of young people around, and most of them seem to know who Yan is and what e:merge is. Yan seems to have good relationships with them too – knows how to connect. But we don't seem to talk about God very much.

I said to Yan, 'Why don't we tell the kids about God? Why aren't we praying for them? Surely we're here to bring the hope of God into this area, and salvation into these kids' lives?' He just said, 'You can pray for them if you want, Niki. I won't stop you.' It felt like he was very comfortable telling them about the project, but wasn't really used to actually telling them about God. I mean, it's all very well doing good work and giving the kids somewhere to go, but if they don't know that Jesus has saved them, what's the point?

None of the staff at the centre even seem to talk about Jesus very much. It's a bit odd. It's not youth work as I know it. A couple of them smoke, too. They go outside to do it, but still, they smoke by the front door, where everyone comes in. I'm not sure it gives a very good impression.

Yan

In the beginning, when we arrived in this place it took some time to work out how to relate to the kids and keep control. There was no pattern or model that we could use to work with the communities we found here. Nothing of what we had previously done fitted, so we had to make it up. We struggled quite a bit to create order within the drop-in centre. The young people were often violent or abusive, and because I was in charge, the senior person and also quite big, when they reached the age of fifteen or so, they would start on me. They would target me – a bit like goats, trying to show off to each other by fighting the biggest one around – and it was out of control. So at various stages I actually had to carry young people out of the building, to stop them destroying the centre, or attacking other kids or my staff. It's not good youth work practice, but that's what I did.

At one point, there was a lad called Mike who came to the centre. He was extremely disruptive, and on one occasion, he disrupted everything to the point of violence, breaking the equipment, stopping the kids from playing pool and threatening the staff. I asked him on numerous occasions to leave. He just point-blank refused and said to me, 'Make me! Go on, make me leave!' He had this snide look on his face, and it really got to me. So eventually I did have to make him leave. I had to pull him up from the chair and practically carry him to the door to make him go. All through this he was shouting abuse at me – using really horrendous, violent language. I managed to keep my mouth shut, though, and was using the minimum of physical force that was necessary just to remove him from the premises, for the safety of the other young people and the staff.

As he was at the door, shouting all this abuse at me, I struggled really hard to maintain my composure and not get rough with him. Then he thrust his face right in mine, yelling abuse at me, and suddenly I couldn't help it. I absolutely lost it. I yelled at him, screaming as I threw him out of the door, completely losing my temper and saying things I should never have let myself say. I was so furious with him, and I couldn't keep myself together. You could see the lad was stunned for a second at my reaction. He'd never seen me like that – none of them had – and he was quite frightened of me all of a sudden. He turned and left, running away and shouting over his shoulder that he would call his parents and report me to the police.

As soon as he'd gone, I felt awful. There was a hush in the centre and people were just kind of looking at me. I couldn't believe I had allowed myself to lose my temper in that way. I was so angry and frustrated with kids like Mike ruining the very thing we'd set up to help them, I did it in the heat of the moment.

But I knew that was no excuse. I was meant to be the responsible one, the person who showed a better way to do things – the leader of a project that was receiving a lot of financial backing from a lot of very good-hearted people. And yet here was me, shouting and screaming and threatening one of the people I was meant to be helping. To say it's not good youth work practice is a complete understatement. It was an abuse of my power and even of my physical size in terms of knowing that I could intimidate and frighten him if I wanted to.

The following week, I went over to another community facility where I knew Mike would be. There was a big room full of young people and he was there. I went and spoke to the worker in charge. I said to her, 'Can I have a word with the young people?'

She looked at me and said, 'Oh yeah, I heard about you abusing Mike at your project,' but she let me speak to them.

I stood up, and in front of the rest of the group of young people I said to Mike, 'Mike, I just want to say that I'm really sorry for the other night. I'm really sorry that I lost my temper with you. My actions were completely out of order. What you did was wrong, and I did need to get you out of the building, but I am sorry for the way I did it. I apologise.'

Even though many people here have quite topsy-turvy lives, they still have a strong sense of justice. Something about me going there and saying sorry created a sense among the young people of, 'OK, he screwed up, but he admitted it. He said sorry. Fine, let's move on.' They really know what it is to screw up. They know what it's like to do something you regret. Also, they often get abused by adults, and around here, young people pretty much have to take whatever they get from adults. But here was an adult saying, 'I'm sorry, I shouldn't have done that to you.' They don't hear that very often.

They listened and there was a kind of connection there. A bit of respect came out of it – a bit of good feeling and relationship between all of us. Mike even came over and shook my hand at the end, which was astonishing. I'm not saying we were suddenly best of friends, but it was almost as if, seeing that I, too, made a mess of things but had the strength to admit it rather than try and cover it up or run away, made him feel we were not so much on different sides.

There are plenty of moments when I've screwed up, in all sorts of ways, but it's OK. You say sorry, you start again. I don't say it's right to screw up, but somehow within this community, you seem to get forgiven more quickly. Screwing up is what they're used to, and admitting you were wrong is rare, especially for an adult. It says in Romans 5:20 that where sin abounds, grace abounds even more. Perhaps it's that.

Niki's diary, 27 April 2005

My 'Boppit' got thrown in the bin today. I had it for drop in, because I thought the kids would enjoy it. They did at first – they were all having a go playing with it – and then somebody got irritated with it, and so they threw it away. They didn't ask me or anything. That was a non problem kid, too. I couldn't believe it! Everything's so immediate here, and there's no sense of respecting other people's things. It was just like, if something's annoying me, I throw it in the bin. Full stop.

It took a while, but I made them get it back out for me.

Yan

Everything's very much in the moment here. It can be quite mad. You can't say, 'This is what will happen next' or 'This is why someone did such and such' – it's too spontaneous – not always in a good way! One time, there was a group of really difficult lads coming to the centre. They were real trouble. Like a pack of dogs, if you touched one of them, they'd all be on you. They were causing havoc in the centre, so I just had to get them out. I got hold of one of them, holding his arms to restrain him, and put him out of the centre. I was trying to stay aware of what was going on around me, because I knew the others would want to try and get me. Just as I put this lad out of the front door, I looked round and somebody ran past me with a pool ball and whacked me straight in the eye with it.

I collapsed in a heap on the ground with blood everywhere. Two of the project volunteers tried to chase the guys but they couldn't catch them. I was taken to hospital and had to have stitches under my eye. It was pretty bad.

For months afterwards, they avoided me like the plague. We just didn't see them around. But about 2 years later, I started to see the lad who had hit me with a pool ball in our area. Then one night completely out of nowhere, he walked up to me in the street and said, 'Yan, I've become a Christian.' I was gobsmacked. We hadn't seen him at our centre, but he had obviously become a Christian elsewhere, through other people, and he wanted to come and tell me. I could hardly believe it. It was amazing!

I'm not saying everything was perfect for him after that – it wasn't – but things do turn around. Sometimes it takes years, and sometimes it's when you least expect it, and sometimes you don't even know it has happened. But it taught me a good lesson – things do turn around.

3

Short Skirts and New Coat Hooks

Niki's diary, 24 May 2005

I've been here about five weeks now, and all I get from the young people is criticism. They mostly call me a geek or chavvy. How ironic is that! 'Geek' because I'm educated and middle class I think. 'Chavvy' because I dress differently to them. But I can't try and be what I'm not, and I'm certainly not going to change my style of dress to fit in better with how they think I should look.

Yan and Sharon have been here for twelve years I discovered today. They have decided to live here and bring up their children here. They have a son and a daughter – Ben is eight and Esther is five. I suppose, even though I still don't really understand the way they operate, I can see their love for this place and the people here. They're very faithful.

Three of the lads were really annoying yesterday. They pulled off all the coat hooks that we'd put up in the entrance. About twenty of them. They were mounted on this long piece of wood and the lads yanked the whole thing down, just leavhg a massive hole in the plaster. It's so meaningless. They didn't even try and get away with it. And it was a really nice touch to have those coat hooks – it was a suggestion from one of the young people, and everyone had chosen the hooks together so there would be somewhere to hang coats and jackets. But even though they were there for the young people's benefit, with these three lads, it was as though they just had to destroy them.

One of them was Dennis and we thought we'd actually had a good session with him at drop in that day, then he went and did that. Sharon has asked me to go and see his mum because we'll have to ban him for a while, and we'll have to explain that to her.

I don't think there's anything here, in terms of deprivation, that I didn't see to some degree when I worked in Devon, or even in Macclesfield. The thing is though, elsewhere, I saw pockets of it. Here, it's everywhere. It's the scale that's different. It does my head in.

Yan

Sharon and I weren't personally shocked by the deprivation here in its simplest sense. We had worked in squats and with drug addicts and prostitutes when we were in Montreal. Sharon was born in Britain, but brought up in various countries in Africa. I'm South African through and through. In Africa there is real poverty – literally not enough to eat and no clean water to drink. So this wasn't anything like that. But what shocked us were things like reading levels among young people being so low in a first world country in the twenty-first century. Also, the amount of unemployment and disaffection, and the lack of any real social fabric in the families and communities here. We were also surprised that so many people here had never heard anything at all about Jesus.

In quite a few larger families in this area, no two children have the same dad, and no one thinks that that is at all out of the ordinary. One ten-year-old girl we knew was one of three kids with the same mum. Her mum had never married her dad, and had then started a relationship with another man, whose ex-wife had been her best friend and with whom he already had several children. Another local mum slept with her son's best friend as a gift to him for his sixteenth birthday. She got pregnant – by her son's classmate.

The children's sense of identity can be severely undermined. There is a lack of discipline, respect and structure in family and community life. Everything is twisted. Early on, I remember an older teenage girl suddenly clicking that Sharon and I were married. We didn't have any children then, and she couldn't understand that we would have got married before having children. She said to Sharon, 'Where are your kids? Have you left them in South Africa? Why are you married if you have no kids?' I think she thought people only considered getting married when they discovered they were pregnant.

Everything is a crisis. Families often just live from one emergency to the next, with a mountain of unresolved issues they are forever trying to scale. Every so often, it all just erupts.

A young couple were living in a flat across the road from us. There were two children – a boy and a girl – living with them. They were her children. I don't know whether they were his or not. The woman had lived there on her own for some time with the oldest child before the birth of the baby girl. We woke up one night at about 4 a.m. to the sound of smashing glass. At first we thought one of our windows had been broken so we went to investigate. We went up to check our children's windows, and as we checked the front of the house, we could see police officers and cars in the street below.

At this point we also became aware of yelling from the road outside. The police cars were positioned so that they blocked off the section of road immediately outside our house and for about forty or fifty metres in each direction. Two other police cars were parked directly opposite our house, outside the entrance to the block of flats this couple lived in. Then we saw that the man was on the flat balcony, flinging various objects, in an attempt to hit the cars. He was yelling, and was clearly in a lot of pain. We saw pots and pans and some kitchen stuff and a small table being thrown down. Suddenly he disappeared, and then reappeared with the baby girl in his arms. She was one year old.

He was shouting that he would kill himself and the children, too, if the police attempted to enter the flat. We could see police crouching in the stairwells and on the landing outside his front door. Suddenly, while he was still occupied on the balcony, a policeman ran down the stairwell carrying the little boy – a three-year-old. They must have entered the flat while he was distracted, and grabbed the boy. He was still hanging on to the baby as he stood on the balcony.

When he realised what they had done, he went inside and smashed up the interior of the flat. Legs of chairs, a portable TV, clothing and pulled-down curtains all came flying through shattered windows, falling onto the pavement below.

After a bit, the steady stream of raging quietened and for some time there was no movement or sound. At this point the police knocked on our neighbour's front door and asked for permission to enter their house and take up a viewpoint from their front bedroom window which looked directly into the flat. They were concerned that he might be harming the baby or himself.

The major action was over at this point. There was nothing to see any more, and we later heard that the guy handed himself in at about 7 a.m. It took us a while to settle Ben, who had been woken by the shouting and the blue police car lights flashing in his bedroom. We don't know what happened to that guy, or the rest of the family. They have never returned to the flat. And sadly, although this incident was disturbing, we couldn't say that it was completely unusual or even surprising. Those flats have a reputation for antisocial behaviour, and the buildings are thankfully now being done up. The stairwells at that time were shockingly dirty and covered in graffiti. A couple of years earlier, a man was stabbed in the block next door and crawled all the way down the stairs, bleeding, to get out to the phone box to call an ambulance.

We know that some people housed in those flats need support in living in the community. Sometimes they are people with psychiatric disorders. There are a few families who are raising children there and genuinely doing their best – I feel for them, because they have no real alternative for accommodation. I think that people who live in these kinds of conditions, with such poor quality of life and regular disruption around them, are under enormous strain. I don't know how they do it really.

But regarding this incident, one thing in particular struck us. The baby girl, during the whole length of the

incident, didn't cry at all. I remember Sharon saying
to me, 'That is not normal.' Our children would have
been so distressed and frightened by the shouting and
raging, and stuff being smashed – but the baby didn't
show any of this kind of fear or anxiety. It was almost
like she was used to it.

Niki's diary, 27 May 2005

I'm not sure what I'm here for to be honest, and
I feel a bit invisible. John does the Academy.
Yan does all the drop in and detached work, and
is in charge. Sharon is the pastoral leader and
delivers all the personal education and a lot of the
communication skills. Diarmuid turns everything
into a spreadsheet or a business plan and gets
the money to run the project. Sarah shouts at
people who need shouting at. And I'm just Niki. I
haven't really got a role.

It's completely differently run from other places
I've worked. I mean, some of it's good – more
professional. They paid me relocation expenses,
and they give me a proper salary, and a pension,
and a decent contract and stuff. That's all great,
and it makes you feel like at least someone
recognises you're doing a proper job. But I think
what I find hard is that we seem to have more
business meetings than prayer meetings. Maybe
it's because I'm single, but I feel really quite alone.
I miss my parents, too. Living close to them in
Macclesfield was great – being able to pop along
for a chat with Mum whenever I liked.

The kids here find it really weird that I don't
have children. They think I'm too old not to have

a boyfriend and some kids. I'm only twenty six! My friends from university think I'm too <u>young</u> to be thinking about marriage and children! Not here. I was talking to Kirsty the other day – she's a fourteen year old girl I've recently met – and we were talking about relationships and stuff. I told her I didn't want to have sex before I got married and she couldn't believe it. She was completely disgusted. She just looked at me in absolute shock, like I was a total freak, and said, 'Do your parents know?!'

Now she's trying to find me a man! She's not doing it out of friendship really, more that she's so freaked about me she feels I need to be taken in hand and normalised – so it's hardly flattering! But at least she's asking me a lot about God, too. I think it's because she finds my lifestyle so extraordinary – she's trying to figure it out. She'll ask me something about God and then start giving me advice on blokes. She'll say, 'How can you talk to God when you can't see him?' and then, 'You should wear a shorter skirt, Niki, that would help you find a man.' It's hard to know where to start with explaining that actually I'm not interested in just trying to find the first male who comes along. She doesn't seem to get the concept of a soulmate. But then, Kirsty lives with her aunt, because her mum is a prostitute.

Yan

John was organising a trip, and this young lad Paul was coming. His parents had agreed, but they hadn't filled in the consent form so John went round to see this lad to get the form. As John walked up to the house, suddenly Paul came flying round the side of the house and past him. Straight after him came his dad, chasing him with a kitchen knife, going, 'Come back here, you little . . . !' He was calling his son the sort of names that would get you thrown out of a benefits office, let alone a church.

John knew the dad, too, and sort of said, 'Whoa! What's happening here? How are you doing?'

The dad pulled up sharply, 'Yeah, I'm all right,' still waving the knife around.

'Can you put that away, do you think?'

The dad looked down at his hand. 'Oh yeah, sorry.'

He then went into the kitchen and put the knife away. A couple of moments later, Paul was back, they'd kind of forgotten it all, and his dad signed the consent form for the trip.

Often there's little structure at home – no proper discipline or appropriate boundaries. The sense of parental wisdom and responsibility seems to have broken down over generations. When we meet these kids, at ten to eighteen years old or so, many of them are petty criminals – rude, unhelpful, difficult, unstable, aggressive, violent. A few years ago, they were young children. At five or six, they are totally seen as victims. In a few years time, they'll be the parents – and then people will blame them for their children not being brought up well. Right now, they're somewhere in between. It's such a vicious circle. We're not only working against the difficulties that an individual child has in their life, we're working against the difficulties that the child's parents and grandparents and probably great-grandparents have had. It's generational deprivation.

Soon after we'd arrived (while we were living in the

Vine), I was getting a lift home with someone from a meeting we'd been to, and as we came into my road, I saw this kid dancing on my car roof. Just a kid, ten or eleven years old, kind of shaking his body about and dancing on the car roof. He was a pretty good dancer, but he was doing it on my car roof, making great big dents! So I got out of my friend's car and I walked across the street. The kid jumped off and ran behind a building, so I went to fetch him out. I managed to, but he was attacking me, and as I walked across the car park I was holding him at arm's length, to prevent him from kicking and hitting me.

I tried to talk to him, saying, 'What is this all about? Why are you dancing on my car?'

The kid wouldn't admit anything, just whined and all he could say was, 'I'm gonna call my dad, I'm gonna call my dad.'

So I said, 'Fine!' and I actually walked with him to his house to tell his dad.

'Look, your kid was dancing on my car. It's not on. What are you gonna do about it?'

Back then, I expected his dad to be cross with the kid, to apologise to me, and to discipline his son. When I look back, I kind of laugh and think, *wow, was I really that naïve?*

The first thing the kid said to his dad was, 'He got hold of me! He was dragging me!' even though I wasn't hurting him in any way, and was actually just making sure that his punches didn't land on my body while I walked to his house with him.

But of course all his dad was concerned about was how I'd supposedly got hold of his son. He didn't even want to hear about the car, which was how it all started. He wouldn't even acknowledge it. He just called the police and reported me for abuse to his child.

So the police came, we explained to them what had happened and they ended up giving me a verbal warning. I couldn't believe it! Not a caution or anything – it doesn't go on record, and it doesn't mean you've actually done something wrong – they just say, 'Don't do it again.' I think they felt they had to do something.

But I was really angry about it. I mean, how are you supposed to deal with a kid jumping about on the roof of your car? You've taken him to his dad expecting that the dad would be bothered about it but hey, it's not his property, so why would he care? And although he is obviously not supervising his son properly, still, when a stranger gets involved, he gets aggressive and defends his son, even though his son is in the wrong. It's as though, even when they are in a mess, the family is all they have. It's all they know, so they hang on to it and defend it against anyone considered an outsider, even when it's them who are in the wrong.

Another young man we worked with had a fantastically positive relationship with his dad – they were real friends and gained a lot of emotional companionship from each other. However, they were both drug users. The father had so many issues of his own that even though he retained his relationship with his son, he just couldn't be the best role model. They would hang out a lot, and that would include using drugs together. The father was in and out of prison an awful lot for various petty thefts and drug-related offences. When he was in prison and couldn't spend time with his son, his son would really suffer from the loss of that relationship, and you could see him struggling to maintain any emotional stability. It was very difficult to watch that happening, and it was really despite the best efforts of the father, but he was just in too deep to be able to help his son.

One of the most tragic episodes we've known was after Sharon and I had been here a couple of years or so. Sharon's parents were staying with us so we were sleeping in the living room on the sofa bed. At about three in the morning, there was a really loud, desperate hammering and ringing of our doorbell. We went to the door, and it was a girl we'd been working with since we'd arrived in Bradford. She was sixteen or seventeen, and had frequently come to the drop-in sessions we ran. She had not long since had a baby. The father was about nineteen and was a heroin addict.

So she's standing there on our front step, hammering at the door in an absolute state, and she says, 'You have to pray for me.' The father of her baby had just died. He had been stabbed by his best friend. They'd had a fallout about some money and drugs and the friend had stabbed him. Because he was a drug user, when they got him on the operating table the medical staff could not stop him bleeding. So he died on the operating table. Nineteen years old.

He was a user, and he was often mean to her. He'd got her hooked on drugs as well, and the whole situation was an absolute mess, but nevertheless, he was the only kind of partner she had – he and their baby were the only people she could call family, and then he was taken away from her.

Niki's diary, 29 May 2005

Dennis came up to me at Xstream on Friday and said, 'Can we please go out and have a one to one? I need to talk to you, please can we go out?' He's never done that before with me at all. He was desperate to talk to someone. We had quite a good chat, about him and those others ripping out the coat hooks, as well as some other stuff. His older brother, who he has always adored, has recently come out of prison and is using a lot of drugs. That day, his brother had come home out of his mind. He had smashed the TV screen and then used a piece of the glass to cut himself, all in front of Dennis. It messed up Dennis's head and he didn't know what to do with it, so he came to e:merge all wound up. Evidently, we managed to entertain him for a couple of hours but then he just flipped, and that's when he went and ripped out the coat hooks.

I was flabbergasted. Poor kid. It does explain his behaviour a bit more, and to be honest, in my mind I was thinking, 'You see your own brother, high on drugs, cut himself in front of you, yet all you've done is vandalise some coat hooks,' and my heart was really melting for him. The resilience is incredible. But even when you know what was behind it, you can't say, oh well, that's alright then. Their behaviour has to have consequences – and no one else in his life is really giving him a sense of boundaries and consequences. So we banned him for two weeks. When I went round to see his mum to explain, she was supportive. And Dennis understands too. I think he's scared that he doesn't know how to stop being naughty. He's only twelve years old.

It makes you realise, our parents are the people that give us the keys to the rest of our lives. However you see your parents behaving, the chances are that's all you know, and you will end up being like that yourself. There's a big lack of knowledge about positive parenting from generations back. It's as though no one's ever intervened, no one's ever said, 'It doesn't have to be like this.'

John told us a story from when he took the lads to the summer sports camp a few years ago. There was a young boy called Jonny who came up to John at the end of the weekend, and kind of frowned, as though he'd made a discovery that he still didn't quite understand. He said to John, 'You know what I really notice about Christians? What I really like?'

'What's that?' John asked.

'Well, the married couples, they seem to get on. It's like they're married, but they're friends as well.' He paused, considering. 'It's quite good, that.'

4

Hide and Speak

Niki's diary, 10 June 2005

It's hard to adjust to the way the staff and the young people relate to each other here. It's not like, 'I am the youth worker, you are the youth'. There isn't that separation – everyone's in it together. And that's quite intense, because the staff and the kids see you all the time, just as you are. There's no sense of you acting with your professional hat on, then leaving for the day to take it off when you get home. Before, when I was doing lots of youth clubs and schools work, it really felt like I was the hero as soon as I arrived somewhere. If you're doing an assembly, say, you kind of zip in and zap the kids and get really energetic, and then you zoom off again. It's like you're fantastic – from the minute you've walked in the door, they love you: 'Oh, you're the youth worker, oh, you're really cool and you can do clubs and everything and la la la'. They all trusted and liked me from the start because of my job title. But then, I was never involved in their lives. People only saw me being the fun and funky youth worker. They didn't see the normal Niki, the way she is when she gets out of bed every day.

Here, you can't hide anything – I mean, nothing at all. Everything is in your face. I was off for the day yesterday because I had a dicky tummy, and today I told someone that's what I had, and they just went, 'Ew! Diarrhoea!' and then in a flash, everybody knew about it and were all asking, 'So how's your diarrhoea, Niki?' whenever they saw me. And the kids would notice when I went to the loo and when I came out, they would go, 'Was that bad again? Is it all right now?' Honestly! There's no privacy!

Yan

People like John and me get frustrated with Christians not telling it like it is – using spiritual language, and skirting around things they don't really feel comfortable talking about. As though Jesus ever did that! Round here, anything goes. No question can't be asked. Early on, John was leading a Bible study, about relationships and Sharon was there, too. The kids were getting to know John and sussing him out. He wasn't married then, and so they were asking him lots of questions about the idea of not having sex before marriage. Then one of them suddenly turned to Sharon and asked, 'When Yan masturbates, do you watch?'

One of the volunteer leaders who worked with us had to leave after that little incident. He couldn't hack it. Sharon just said, 'That's not really an appropriate question because that's to do with my personal life, so I'm not going to answer it.' But once I'd worked here a

little while, I got to love the honesty. People vote with
their feet here. They're not polite for the sake of it. Not
at all.

Even on the street. People don't stop and think,
'Hang on, who might hear me?' they just say what
they have to say, when it comes into their head, and
in a loud voice. After John was married, he and his
wife Rachel lived in the flat above the Vine centre,
and Sharon and I moved out with our new baby Ben
into a small house. John and Rachel were in bed and
got woken up at something like six in the morning by
shouting outside, between a young man and woman,
both about nineteen or twenty. The lad was running
down the street after her and they could hear both of
them yelling. The lad just shouted down the street at
top volume: 'You shagged my brother!'

Rachel and John couldn't believe it. It's like, hey,
if that had happened to me, I definitely wouldn't be
shouting it out for everyone to hear! Then they started
being afraid for the woman's safety, because they could
hear the guy running after her, still shouting. But before
they had time to get up and look out of the window,
they heard him yell at her once more, just as loud, but
more plaintively this time: 'Can't we just start again?!'

What I've learnt to love about this community, even
from those early days, is the honesty. OK, I don't
mean that people don't steal things or whatever, but
the people in this community are straight with you.
They will call you names and abuse you and shout
and swear, but they don't hide. They are themselves.
They do what they have to do in the moment, and then
it can be forgotten just as quickly. They don't scheme.
I'm a direct sort of person. I don't like trying to work
people out, having to guess what they think of me, or
not knowing where I stand. People here are messed

up, like we all are, and probably more so, but they are direct and up front. It can come as a bit of a shock if you're used to euphemism and social niceties, but me, I've come to like the directness. I can work with that, and I reckon God can, too.

Niki's diary, 16 June 2005

Whenever we come back from detached work, Yan does a kind of debrief, and it's really harsh! He just comes straight out with things like, 'That was no good, the way we approached that group of young people,' or 'That leaflet we gave out looks rubbish – we should redesign it.' He doesn't beat about the bush at all. He does say positive things, too, about what went well, and it's not that any of it is inaccurate, it's just very in your face, especially when he turns to me and says, 'What do you think, Niki?' and I don't know what to say.

I really don't know whether I want to stay here beyond the year that I promised myself. It is so hard to feel like I'm making any difference. Also, I'm lonely. Although some of the other staff are not married, they have closer friends here – people they've known a long time. I feel like I have no one I can talk to at the end of my working day.

Every time 'Youthwork' magazine comes out, I find myself flicking straight to the jobs pages. I haven't applied for any yet, it's more psychological. I think to myself, 'I'm not stranded here – if I want to leave, I can just go and get one of these youth worker jobs advertised by a church.' It helps me not feel trapped.

Yan

Diarmuid had two IT contractors come to e:merge once
to install a new system for us. They were from London
and when they saw our building and the area, they
said to Diarmuid, 'This place is like Beirut. We didn't
think places like this existed in the UK.' They were
really astonished.

Of course it's not really like Beirut – or Somalia – or
all sorts of places in the world where people are a lot
worse off, but the IT guys' reaction shows that the gap
between the comfortable areas and the hard areas of this
country is still dramatic enough to surprise people. This
is a harsh environment and we have trouble recruiting
people to come and work at the project. It's not the
sort of place you'd choose if you wanted an easy life.
It's not the sort of place you can happily invite your
family to visit, and a lot of people don't understand
our work here, which makes many of us feel isolated.
I'd say most of the staff here have thought about giving
up at some point. A few of them *have* given up. One of
the main reasons is that it takes a long time before you
see any results. You don't walk in and achieve your
objective, get job satisfaction immediately, move on.
Not at all. It's hard because it's a slog. It's all about
perseverance, and it affects your faith, too.

If we're not careful, sometimes within our environment
we can become disillusioned because every day we face
the same stuff and, over a long period of time, we can
easily start to think, 'Can Jesus really change things?
Can he really affect people's lives here? Because I don't
see him doing it right now.' Somehow deep down we
know he can, but we don't see the reality of that every
day or even every month – so often for long periods of
time we carry on what we're doing whilst waiting to

see the results. Just digging the soil. Trying to remain faithful.

Sharon and I had been here ten, nearly eleven years when we recruited Niki, and that was a massive milestone. A real highlight. She was the first person we recruited from outside. John, Diarmuid and I had known each other before, and other people we recruited as volunteers had come to us through connections, because frankly, it's hard to get people, so we've essentially had to headhunt. But Niki came from nowhere. She responded to the advert in *Youthwork* magazine. She was the first person we recruited after becoming an independent charitable organisation and calling ourselves e:merge.

We didn't recruit Niki lightly. We thought about it for some time, we discussed it a lot. Niki was a strong candidate. She had experience of Christian youth work. She was well educated. She could tick all the basic boxes – timekeeping, organisational skills, self-motivated. And she did a great presentation which she'd clearly prepared, much better than the other candidates we saw. She could communicate well, but more than anything, I think there was a desire in her to serve and to make a difference in our world, and that is a key quality within our work. We could see that she had a genuine heart for young people – which is crucial when everything else is getting worn down, because without it you can't survive.

I think it was important that she came back and saw the project for that day. John and Sharon and I spent a morning with her discussing things – her asking us questions, us asking her questions – really explaining how things are, some of the issues we face. We didn't want her to come thinking that it was going to be easy. Sharon drove her round the area and explained some of the history of the project and so on, so she knew. As much as we could be, we were honest and upfront and then left the rest to her.

So Niki arrived, with all her spiritual optimism, and it created a kind of a dual effect for the rest of the staff already here. In one sense she was a real breath of fresh air, like a reminder that we do believe in an all-powerful God, a loving God who can and wants to intervene in people's lives. But then again, there was a sense that, you know, once she's been here for a while, it will rub off. She will see that things just aren't that easy. She'll have to ditch some of that excitement and get down to the grind of it. That's quite sad, to have become that cynical.

You can't prepare people for the reality they'll face here. You can't say, 'Look, you're going to see horrible things that you wish didn't exist. It's going to trouble you and you won't know the answers, and sometimes you'll doubt everything you ever believed in.' You can't do that because it's patronising to the person and to the community here, and also because it's not real. They have to see and experience it themselves.

So what I tried to do in those early days was to simply talk with Niki. We would go out on detached work, we'd have conversations about what we saw and I purposely introduced her to really interesting characters in the community so that she could start to form her own opinions. The first reaction of most people is usually: this is too much – it's just too hard. But then after a little time here they see the relational aspect of our work in this community. They see the generosity of people here and they become hooked. It's a combination of that and the need. I think that was the thing with Niki. Although we had concerns maybe about how she would react with the realities of this kind of area, we saw in her someone who had a really genuine heart. So we took the gamble because if you get someone whose heart is right, and they see the need, well, they normally have to stay.

For Diarmuid it happened one morning not long after he had moved here. He was coming out of his flat to go to work. Half past eight on a Monday morning and it was raining. He heard screaming. Lying in the gutter, a few paces from his home, he saw a young woman. She looked to be in her early twenties, had straggly hair, soaked through by the rain, no shoes, unable to stand up. She was high on drugs and screaming in distress. In her confusion she was calling for her mum. 'Mum! Where are you? Mum!' Then he saw a three-year-old girl – the daughter presumably – who was toddling around near the young woman. The young woman caught sight of the girl and started kicking her. Lying in the gutter, yelling for her mum, kicking her own small daughter, absolutely out of her mind.

What do you do? Where in the Bible can you find a nice explanation of why that happens, or a clear instruction of exactly what action you should take? You can't. All you know is that God wants things to get better for people. We all need something beyond ourselves to get us out of the mess we are in.

Niki's diary, 23 June 2005

I sat through the whole of drop in today without saying more than 'hello' to any of the young people. Two and a half hours. Last week, I tried really hard to be friendly and ask questions, but I could tell I was coming across as a bit intense, intimidating them all, and they didn't engage with me. So this week, I thought, 'Well, I'll just be around, but I won't force anything, and if they want to talk to me, they can.' So I sat on the chairs, leafed through a magazine. I cleared some of the cups away, made some tea. I just kept asking, 'You all right?' to whichever young person I was walking past, and they just went, 'Yeah' and carried on with what they were doing. I felt like such a lemon. Honestly, I didn't do a thing. Then as I came out of the kitchen at the end, one of the girls was saying to another, 'It's Niki – yeah – she's a youth worker I think . . .'

They don't even know who I am.

5

Pack Away the Parachute

Yan

It is our experience that when you are dealing with issues and problems that have accumulated over generations, even the best projects and charities cannot make a substantial difference in a short time. If there's anything Sharon and I have learned from being here it's that we're not dealing with quick fixes. We're dealing with entrenched difficulties and long-term problems that require long-term solutions. And if you want to be part of a long-term solution in an area like this, you have to get involved. You have to get your hands dirty. You have to stay.

When Sharon and I arrived here in 1994, there was no youth provision at all, and no resources to provide it. Our first achievement was a table tennis table – or rather, a board of MDF with lines we painted on it, balanced on a folding table. We'd come from Montreal, where we had been training with Operation Mobilisation. I had asked Sharon to marry me, and part of that meant discussing the kind of life we would have together. Not a normal one in many ways.

We'd met in South Africa, where we both grew up. I was a policeman and she was a teacher, but we both felt a call to mission and I knew I wanted to work in inner-city areas and with young people. So I worked with Operation Mobilisation for a year, and then went to get trained by them in Montreal. On the way to Montreal I called in on Bradford for a summer city mission.

I was placed in a small inner-city church in Bradford 4 where the minister knew that he wanted to provide something for young people. During those two weeks, I saw the people and the dedicated minister trying to make a difference in a needy place with a couple of committed volunteer staff. I think they could see that it was making an impact on me. One of them said to me, 'Why don't you go and get your OM training for two years, and then come back and be the youth worker here?' I just sort of chuckled. Two years later, I had my training, Sharon and I had started dating, and were talking about life together, and I wrote to the minister in Bradford, just to see what was going on there. He wrote back. Turned out the church had just bought a building that it wanted to turn into a community centre and were looking for a full-time youth worker to start later in the year. We called in on Bradford together before going back to South Africa for our wedding. We agreed to think and pray about the position. We got married in April and arrived here in September.

I'm not sure what expectations I had when I got here. I'm not a big expectations person. It's more that the area had stayed in my mind, because there was so clearly a need. The aim was simply to have a place in the community where young people could go who were between the ages of eleven and twenty-four. I think what I wanted was to see if God could make a difference in an area like Bradford 4. It was a test for myself in a way. I believed God could do anything, did I? Did I believe that if I let God work in me, he could make a difference in an area as seemingly hard as BD4? If so, was I prepared to give him a chance to prove it?

That was twelve years ago. Ask me today whether God can make a difference in an area like Bradford 4 and I'll still give you a reserved answer. Twelve years might be a long time in my life, but compared to how many years this area has been in the grip of deprivation, and how much it needs God to turn things around, it's really not long at all.

Niki's diary, 8 July 2005

Sometimes I feel like I'm starting to relate to the kids, and sometimes I feel like I'm getting nowhere. Sharon told me last Thursday that Claire had come up to her during drop in and said, 'Niki's well ace.' That was pretty encouraging, because she's always so quiet and if anything, kind of critical or negative. It's a shame she can't say it to my face of course, but there you go.

Then today, Julie was really weird to me. I don't understand her. We were doing art, and some of us had decided to do these cool collage things we'd seen in a magazine. Julie came up behind me and went, 'That's crap,' then pulled out a felt tip pen and scribbled all over my collage. Then she got hold of the magazine we were using, ripped it in two and dropped it on the floor and walked off. I don't get it at all. She wouldn't say why she did it, just shrugged. The other kids just shrugged, too, picked up the magazine and tried to stick the page back together.

I am so impressed when I look at Yan's and Sharon's commitment to this area. I recognise the missionary heart in them, because this is mission and they are here for the long run. They've stayed here and they're raising their children here – have done for the last twelve years. That's serious commitment – that's not me going, 'I'll see if I can hack it for a year!'

The young people here know it, too. They know Yan and Sharon aren't just a flash in the pan – they've literally seen them around the area for years. They know their children. That's what their relationships with the young people are based on. You look at Sharon and you know she's a long term person. She's a discipler. You see her with the young people, and it's like she has sowed the seed, and she is waiting. She is waiting for the truth to sink in, for the light bulb to be turned on, for the harvest to be ready. She's very patient, because she knows it takes time.

I know I have a missionary heart, too – that's what brought me here. But I'm still not sure whether this is really my mission field.

Yan

In order to continue here, you need to, I don't want to use the phrase 'lower your expectations', but perhaps *shift* your expectations. You need to understand that you are here for the long haul. In order to make a real impact on young people's lives here, you're going to have to be around for a decent length of time. You can't parachute in and go, 'Tell me all your problems and I'll help you sort them out,' and then move on in a couple of years' time. You have to pack away the parachute.

People here have been cheated and lied to all their lives. They've been promised things and not seen them delivered. They've learnt not to trust anyone, because that's how they survive. What they need is someone who is there. Someone who is perhaps there for a long time even before starting to preach to them, or starting to challenge them. Someone who is prepared to wait until the young people trust them. That can take a lot of time, but I think God is patient. He knows who we are, he knows what a mess a lot of us are in, and he knows that sometimes it takes ages for us to be ready to respond to him. He waits for us. So we need to be prepared to wait for others as well.

Sharon and I have been here for almost twelve years. We don't think, hey, what shall we do next? What new place could we go to? As long as God keeps giving us vision for this area, and for the work of e:merge, and as long as we know broadly where to take it next, then we are open to being here. If at some point it's very clear that we don't have a clue where it's supposed to go next and we don't have any vision any more, then we'll hand over to somebody else.

I think it's one of the things that makes e:merge very special and different – the fact that we build long term relationships with the young people we serve. We are not just in and out, and we don't treat them as customers, or people we want to deliver a product to. We are saying to the young people, 'you matter, we will walk this road with you'. And we're not only saying that to them verbally, we're saying it through our presence here and by the fact that we've stayed. Through thick and thin we are here. We don't run away when it gets hard. We don't get bored or fed up when it takes longer than we'd like.

It does take a long time to build relationships here because the more hurt a person has been in their life, the more wary they will be opening up to someone new. So you can't arrive and start relating immediately. Especially someone like Niki, who doesn't look or sound like the people kids around here would normally be used to relating to. It will always take a while for any of the kids to trust her or want to work with her. That's just how it is, and that's how it was for all of us. It's hard, though, while you're waiting.

Niki's diary, 15 July 2005

I was talking to Sharon today, and she said she feels alone, too. Even married, and with kids, and settled in a church – she has a sense that people don't understand what she does. That kind of alarmed me – if she feels like that, having Yan's support and having got to know the area and seen changes, no wonder I feel that way, too. But I suppose at least it means it's not just me going quietly mad on my own.

I just want to see a little sign that I'm making a difference. Just a small something that can say, come on Niki, keep going, it's worth being here. It's too hard to carry on with nothing at all.

Yan

Our mission statement is to meet young people at their point of need and to challenge and develop them at all levels. So it's a holistic thing that we do, and it starts not with our agenda, but with where the young person is at and what they need. That sounds obvious I know, but it's amazing how many people think that youth work is all about laying your expectations on the young people and expecting stuff of them, regardless of who they are, where their life is at, or what their needs are. You wouldn't treat an adult like that. You don't get doctors in hospital administering a medicine before they have talked to a patient and found out what's wrong with them. You seek to understand the person first, and then you're in a place to respond to their needs. And understanding someone takes time.

I think one of the things that enables us to keep going, even when it's hard to see fruit, progress and change, is that we firmly believe that God is a long-term God. What I love about God is that he's not interested in fixing something superficially so it looks pretty and in two years' time collapses again. He's in it for the long haul. God hasn't given up on me, and he's not going to give up on anyone. We can't tell people what to do to sort their lives out. What we can do is show through our lives that the way we live is committed and faithful and that we will stick it out and not abandon the people we work with. Our job is to be constantly faithful, constantly loving, constantly supporting them, unconditionally. If they can believe that people can be like that, they might just believe that God is like that.

I think also, that God in his grace sometimes allows you to see little glimpses, and he allows you to experience the sense that yes, somewhere deep inside a young person, something is happening. So throughout the almost twelve years that we've been here, there have been moments when we have seen a tiny sign that a young person is really moving on in faith. Whether they're from a Christian home or a non-Christian home, and whether they have made a commitment to God or not. You just occasionally see the impact that we have on a life.

One of the young people that we worked with has now just gone to college. Six years ago, that would have been completely unimaginable because he was too disruptive and did not have any sticking power. But now he's there and sticking it out. So you know – yes, we've made a change in his life.

His brother is a Christian, and has also been around for a long time, coming to drop-ins and Xstream. His mother will tell you that if it wasn't for what we've done here, he would not have continued with the faith. Given the pressures in other parts of his life, he would have given up long ago. That's very hard to measure of course, and very hard to prove to anybody, but we know. We know that e:merge has made a difference in his life and that he's going on strong in the faith.

Another young person, from a non-Christian home, started to come to Xstream some time ago, and now she's joined a church – an adult congregation. She is nineteen or twenty. She's never declared that she has become a Christian, but she has enough interest and confidence to go to an adult congregation, so for us that's a big deal. We're blessed by that.

Our aim is to see God transform this community, but at the moment, we look for small signs in young people's lives to see that things are moving in the right direction. The community has been oppressed for generations, so like a supertanker, it takes time to turn around. We believe that those little things are signs that the tanker is slowing down and starting to steer in a different direction. You do have to shift your expectations, but what that should mean, I think, is that we stop saying, 'big things will happen immediately' and we start believing that over a long period of time, even more enormous things will happen.

Over the years, we have often had young people ask us, 'Why are you here? Of all the places you could go, why are you here?'

So we say, 'Well, this is the place that God wants us to be.'

'So do you think God really cares about Bradford then?'

'Well yeah, I do.'

And that surprises them. There's a little tiny light that goes on, and it's those tiny lights that you take to heart and store up for yourself as a way of saying, yes it's taking a long time, but it's happening. We are going the right way. We are making a difference.

Niki's diary, 18 July 2005

One of our young people got stabbed at the weekend. He was walking home in the evening, so it was dark, and this group of lads who he didn't know came up to him. They said, 'Give us your phone and your money.'

He said, 'No,' and they beat him up. Once they'd kicked him in and he was lying in the gutter, they went off and he managed to drag himself home. He was in a bad way, and he sat on the sofa waiting for his mum to get back home, but thought he had just been kicked and punched. Then he noticed that he was bleeding on the cushion covers. His mum got home, about half an hour later, and had a look, and they realised he'd been stabbed – a big gash in his side. She rang an ambulance and they took him to casualty. He needed seven stitches.

We asked him why he hadn't rung an ambulance straight away after the beating, but he just shrugged his shoulders like it was an irrelevant question.

Life here is not glamorous. Sometimes when people talk or write about 'difficult' young people they glamorise it – they make out there's this mad violence happening all the time, and a kind of gang culture, like the Sopranos or something. They make the young people into really articulate, sort of, genius gangsters who have decided to drop out of society and are making their own, heroic way through life, joyriding Mercedes round council estates. The reality's not like that. Life is not like a soap opera or a gritty drama for the young people here. For some of them, it's a long, hard slog they can only just about manage. For many of them it's bleak, shabby and grim.

6

Happy Families

Yan

Settling in Bradford completely changed our lives. When we first came here, we really weren't thinking, 'this is our life from now on'. We thought we might be here for a few years to help establish the new youth work. Then we realised after three years that really we'd only scratched the surface. So we committed for another three. But we always felt we'd go back to South Africa at some point.

During that second period of three years we felt God challenge us. We went home for a holiday – Ben was about three years old – and we felt God say to us, 'You've always thought you'd go back to South Africa. Are you going to hold me to that? Are you going to continue to hang on to that ideal? Or are you going to allow me to direct your life? Actually surrender? And what if it is Bradford for the rest of your lives? Is that OK? Are you going to be that open to me directing you?'

Sharon remembers very distinctly God saying to her, 'Are you going to opt in, the way the young people here have to opt in?' Because they don't have a choice. The young people who were born here don't have a choice. We can say – if it all goes wrong, if I get fed up with it and don't like it any more, I can always just go somewhere else – but they don't have that option. So God said, 'Are you going to give your life – live your life – for Bradford? Or not?'

In some ways it was an obvious decision. We knew that God is not someone who turns his back on places and people that need him, leaving for somewhere prettier or more comfortable. I think if Jesus lived in England today, he'd be somewhere like this. So when we thought and prayed about it, we knew that committing to Bradford was the right, the good thing to do. But knowing it's the *right* decision doesn't make it an *easy* decision. In terms of the implications, it's a decision that you have to think about thoroughly beforehand because there are costs involved, not just for you but also for your children and wider family. It means we live every day somewhere that is not the most attractive, easy place for us to be. It means we bring our children up in an area that is not the safest place for them. It meant telling our parents that we couldn't say that we would *ever* return to South Africa – never mind when. It was hard to tell them that they might never have regular contact with their grandchildren.

We've lived in the area the whole twelve years we've been here. In fact, where we live now is as far away from the e:merge building as we have ever been. We lived in the flat above the centre for six years when it was called the Vine, and the other five years we lived in a house that was within a stone's throw. This last year, we've moved a bit further away – about a mile – to a house that's a little bigger.

I think Sharon and I both feel that potentially people might judge us and disapprove of the way we have chosen to bring up our children. I'm the last one to say that every youth worker has to bring their children up in the area they work in, but I hope what my children will see above all when they grow up and look back on this time is that their parents did what they did wholeheartedly. I think I would like them to realise that Sharon and I didn't mess around – we didn't claim to be doing good work with people without actually engaging in the area those people lived in. But it does cost.

I went to fetch Ben from school one day, and as we were walking back, only a few metres from our house actually, there was an older teenage lad standing in the path on the pavement with a massive rock, and with no warning he threw the rock at Ben, and only missed him by an inch or two. Ben was about five years old at the time. I couldn't believe it, and I reacted immediately, 'What do you think you're doing? What's going on?' at which point the guy pulled a knife on me, in full view of Ben. He came up towards my throat and was threatening me. It was pretty frightening. I could tell he was high on some kind of drug, so I didn't know what he might do.

I shouted to Ben, 'Run home, run inside,' and he took off with a terrified look on his face, glancing back at me. The knife was so close I couldn't move, but thankfully, someone else had already seen the guy acting threateningly and had called the police. They came round the corner while he still had this knife to my throat. As soon as he saw the police, he took the knife away and ran off so fast that they couldn't catch him.

When I'd finished talking to the police and giving my statement, I went back to my house. Sharon had been standing in the kitchen when Ben ran in – a five-year-old on his own, wide-eyed and panting, and saying, 'Mummy, there's a man outside with a knife and he's pointing the knife at Papa.' We were all quite shaken. That was the first time we had a really nasty incident which Ben witnessed, so we had to talk it through with him for some time. He was asking all the questions – 'Papa, why did that boy want to hurt you? What did he want to do to you?'

We said that we thought the lad was probably in a very difficult period of his life and that he would be sorry one day when he realised what he had done. We also said that it was very possible that the lad had been taking drugs and didn't really know what he was doing. Also, that when people were sad and desperate they also became angry, and sometimes when people are angry they can do things that later they regret. That's how we talked to him about it, and it was definitely a good thing that we tried to answer all his questions and reassure him as much as we could. But at the same time, obviously, you're thinking, what a tragedy that I have to explain this kind of thing to a five-year-old. I wouldn't really want my children to know what it means to be high on drugs until much later in their life, let alone to have witnessed a violent, drug-induced incident. I think that sort of incident could happen to people in all sorts of places, at some point in their lifetime, but it's a lot more commonplace somewhere like this, so you tend to come across it earlier in life – when you're five and walking home from school.

My kids have had to grow up more quickly than a lot of children their age. Ben was nervous of going outside for a little while after that incident, but it passed. And the thing is, he has become very streetwise now. Much more recently, when he was nine or ten years old, he was out playing on his bike with a friend, and he had very fancy wheel caps. He came near a gang of lads and they stopped him and took the wheel caps off his bike and one of the lads pushed him over. Ben was quite brave. He actually stood up to them, and the friend he was with stuck by him, too. Even though they were bigger than Ben, he was very much saying, *You're not allowed to do that, you cannot do that, it's not right.* He wasn't scared of them. I was pleased about that. You need a bit of guts to survive here – and a few good, brave friends. We teach him not to back down, not to be afraid of confrontation, but of course to recognise when he is in actual physical danger. We teach our children to be peace-loving first and foremost, of course. But we also teach them not to be pushovers. After all, they are children of the King of Kings and the Almighty God.

Ben has actually grown up much bolder and less scared than he might have done in a safer place. There are two sides to that. It's a good thing that he's streetwise, but it's a terrible shame that he has to be.

I think the thing about bringing up children is felt even more keenly by Sharon. She did some real heart searching about it when we were deciding to settle here, but she feels now that God is with her and supporting her through all these issues. She has two close friends who are also South African, both teachers, from similar backgrounds, living elsewhere in the UK. They each have children as well. Both of them are teaching at private schools and their children have assisted places. I think when she's with them, she's very aware that maybe their children are having educational opportunities that ours aren't. You know, even if we wanted to, we couldn't afford to send our children to a private school.

But we wouldn't want to anyway – that's not a choice that anyone in this area has, so why should we?

When we look at our children, not only are they much more streetwise but they are also much more able to cope with a wide spectrum of people. We try and keep their experience as wide as possible, because we do have the opportunity to do that. We make an effort to go to different places on holiday and we don't only have friends that are involved in youth work. And of course, we ourselves are from somewhere else, so they visit South Africa with us every few years. They have an extended family that lives abroad; they have a father who speaks a language other than English as his first language and so on. I think my children are quite a lot more tolerant than they would be if they weren't growing up somewhere like BD4. They don't easily make judgements on other people's behaviour.

Both Ben and Esther go to an urban school – the local school – where more than one third of the children are on the Special Needs Register. Most of Ben's friends are from working class households, and a great deal of them are from lone parent families. His class is made up of kids with lots of different religious and ethnic backgrounds. Quite a few of the children have fathers or older brothers who are in prison, or members of the family who have drug or alcohol issues. All those things are now normal for them, so they are accepting of children straight away, whatever they look like and whatever they can or can't do. They don't experience many barriers in relating to people, because they have seen so much.

Ben has never been scared by films and TV that some children can't watch – *Jurassic Park*, or *Dr Who* or whatever. The film that he found the most scary when he was little was *Mrs Doubtfire* because the daddy left.

That was real for him, because a lot of his friends at school have had that happen to them.

Of course, those things happen in suburban areas and affluent society, too. Divorce, drug dependency, alcoholism. The difference is, for the majority of people in the UK, if one thing in your life goes wrong, the rest of your life is stable enough to see you through. You might have the money to check into a clinic, or private health insurance. You probably have a decent home, the motivation to try and address your problems, or at least some reliable friends and family members who themselves have stable enough lives for you to be able to lean on them for a little while. Here, people have fewer resources physically and emotionally to deal with the heartaches and difficulties. All human beings are in essence the same, but I think poverty exacerbates every other problem and issue, making it harder to deal with and making its effects more painful.

We are lucky because the school our children attend is a good one and tries to address the needs of all the children, supporting those who need supporting, stretching those who need stretching. That's far from easy for the school because it doesn't have unlimited resources.

Ben will be starting secondary school next year, so we're having to choose a new school for him and our options are limited. There is a lot of faith in that – trusting that God somehow is going to create the right place for him and we have to trust that if God wants us here, God knows about Ben and is going to look after him as well, but as a parent, you do wonder. I know that Sharon worries about that side of things, but at the end of the day, this is the choice we have made, and we knew what the implications might be. It's a combination of doing everything you can to create the life you want for your children, and then at the same time, having to leave everything to God. So we have to trust God that he knows what Ben's needs are and what Esther's needs are and that he will somehow meet them.

Ben and Esther like where they live – they both greatly enjoy their lives, and we're very grateful for that. If we ever talk about moving they are completely against it, because despite everything else, there's a strong sense of community here that you don't get everywhere. They know they belong here and are really part of something, and we're so grateful for that. There will always be issues to work through – and I suspect with Esther being a girl, there'll be different ones as she gets older – but you take it as it comes, and you trust God to keep seeing you through.

7

You Go First

Niki's diary, 11 August 2005

I was desperately trying to have some conversation with one of the girls the other day, and I knew she had said she liked dancing. I had a leaflet about a funky aerobics class at a gym not far away. I said to her, 'Hey – maybe we should go and check this class out.' But she quickly closed down and said, 'I won't do it. I'm not good at that. I'm not good at new people,' then got up and walked off. It was quite sad really.

It would be easy to be intimidated by some of the young people here because they are full of bluster and seem confident and aggressive, but it's actually a defence thing because their worlds are so small. I guess even if your home situation is not a safe place, it's what you know. Anything outside that is way too scary.

At drop in today, I mentioned to one of the young people that I've done some mime before, and they immediately went, 'Can you do the wall?' So I said yes, and did it, and they were dead impressed. They called some of the others over and said, 'Look, she can do the wall!' and made me do it again. I was a bit embarrassed! After all this time that I've been trying to get the kids interested in knowing about me, finding out who I am, and now they're all really interested because I can do something so simple. It's such a tiny connection, but at least it is a connection! I might start doing some mime workshops with them, or theatre or something.

Yan

John takes a load of lads to a residential, week-long youth camp most summers. It's in North Yorkshire, in a sort of country house activity centre on the edge of quite a posh small town. I mean, isn't just posh for our kids, it's genuinely upper class. John and his wife Rachel were sat round one night, just chatting, and one of the young people from another group, about fourteen years old, was going, 'A friend of mine, they have caviar once a week, but we don't have caviar – not Beluga anyway. We have lumpfish. I don't know why they have caviar when they could have lumpfish because they taste exactly the same and caviar's about £20 for a jar, and lumpfish is only £5 a jar, and tastes just as delicious, so I really don't know why they don't just have lumpfish.' And then he went, 'What do you think, John?'

'Mate,' says John, 'to be honest, I don't have a clue. I've never seen caviar and I've never even heard of lumpfish so I don't know what you're on about.'

John's wife, Rachel, from the other end of the table, tries to help.

'No, John, you have. What's that stuff your sister has when we go out for meals as a starter?'

'That's paté, darling, otherwise known as meat paste, but thanks for your contribution.'

Not all the kids were from a caviar-eating background of course – it was a very mixed camp, so aiming to be very inclusive. It had people from lots of different backgrounds, and both churched and un-churched young people. Nevertheless, we could see that when John decided to take some of our lads there, it was going to be interesting.

He drove them there in the minibus. They were all in the back, big teenage lads, and all the way there, they were going, 'If anyone starts on me, I'm going to proper knack him!' They were asking John, 'What will happen if we scrap with someone?' They were making out that they were ready for a big fight and planning how many of the other kids they were going to nut.

They arrived, and John pulled up to the place where the camp was held and there were loads of kids milling around. They always do the camp really nicely – it's a lovely building, quite grand, and they decorate the entrance so it's very welcoming. There were young people the same age as John's group, in groups or with their parents dropping them off. People were unloading bags, jumping out of cars, generally being cheerful and a bit noisy. So John parks the minibus, and gets his stuff, opens the back of the bus for the lads to jump out: 'Right lads, get your bags, we'll go and register.'

So he gets his bag out and starts walking. He goes about fifty yards before realising there's no one with him. He looks round, and this group of seven big, teenage lads who all the way there have been talking about how much harder they are going to be than the other kids, and how much fighting they're going to do, are cowering in the back of the van, squashed in, not moving. John goes back to the van. It's in silence.

'Lads, what's going on?

Silence.

'Lads, come on, we need to go and register.'

Eventually, 'Go on, Dave, you go first.'

'No way, mate, you go.'

'Uh-uh. I'm not going first.'

They're all petrified. Scared to death. They have never been in a situation like this before, and it's way outside what they know. Even at the age of fifteen or sixteen, it is completely alien to them to go away and mix with people their age who they hadn't met before. Amazingly, some of these lads had probably never left Bradford, never related with people their age who are from different backgrounds, or even different towns. What you don't realise – because it's covered over with all this defensive/aggressive behaviour – is that their comfort zone is very, very small.

Even within e:merge, you talk to the Bradfordian young people who work for us, and they hardly ever leave Bradford. Sarah, when she came to work with us a few years back, would say she didn't really see her aunt and cousins, because they lived way over in Wibsey. Wibsey is the other side of Bradford – about ten or fifteen minutes' drive away. But this aunt and cousins had 'moved away', so the rest of the family don't see them any more. There was another family where the mother wouldn't speak to one of her daughters because she had moved to Leeds. Obviously, Leeds is about twenty-five minutes' drive from here, but the interpretation was that this woman had moved there because she thought she was better than the rest of her family, who still lived in Bradford. They live and die here, in this very small geographical area, and if you ask the kids where they want to live when they're older, they don't really understand the question. 'In Bradford, of course!' They know people here. There's no concept of being able to move. North Yorkshire must have felt like worlds away.

It took a lot of encouragement, but the lads did eventually get out and unpack. And although it was nerve-wracking for them, they got through the week and enjoyed it. In the end, more than a few of them wanted to go back again the following year. It was pretty successful – for nearly all of them.

There was one kid though, Steven, who was twelve at the time. It was obvious he was struggling all week. The meetings and stuff are really geared towards kids that are ready to sit and listen and have an attention span. Steven doesn't have one. One of the team leaders came up to John one afternoon in the middle of a session, a couple of days into the camp, and said, 'John, you're going to have to deal with this. We've found Steven. He's walked out of the meeting, and he's been seen in the middle of town. Up a statue. Swearing at cars.'

So John tears off, and in the middle of this beautiful North Yorkshire market town, with its grand old stone houses, and quiet lanes and thatched cottages, up a splendid raised stone cross slap bang in the middle of the crossroads, there is Steven, swinging out from the statue, yelling every four-letter-word you could imagine at each car that drives past. He's holding on to the statue with one hand, and with the other he's giving the finger to the drivers in the cars, yelling and going absolutely bonkers.

John has to get him down, so he climbs up and wrestles him off the statue, and picks him up and carries him away from it, across the road. Steven is struggling and still yelling and swearing, and hitting

John wherever he can, pummelling him with his fists and his feet. The other youth leaders are sort of tiptoeing alongside, without getting too close, going, 'I'm not sure you ought to pick him up – I mean, you shouldn't really be restraining him.' And John's carrying him while he's punching and kicking, and trying to nut John, just going, 'Mate, if you know a better way, you're welcome to take over . . .'

We had to send Steven home. John said to him, 'Steven, you can't behave like that. You're going to have to go home,' and the lad cried. Even though he couldn't cope with it, he didn't want to be sent home. That was like he'd failed, and besides, he loved being there. He loved it, but it was too much for him to cope with at the same time. So he cried for ages but John had to send him home.

One of the volunteers at the camp, a woman called Joanne, said she'd drive him back to Bradford. So they got in the car, him still snivelling, and Joanne took him off. Ten minutes later, she's on the phone to John, panic in her voice.

'John, I stopped at a red light and Steven bolted. I don't know where he is. He just jumped out of the car and went running up the street.'

So John had to go out and find him again – out around the town looking for a Bradfordian 'delinquent' who may or may not be swearing, running or sticking up the wrong fingers. Who knows whether he was trying to run back to the centre or what – it's never that rational. He couldn't cope so he was just running. He didn't have any other strategy.

In the end, they had to escort him back to Bradford in a van that belonged to another of the leaders, with Joanne sitting in the back with him to make sure he couldn't get out. The saddest thing is that Steven liked it. He wanted to be part of the whole weekend, he really wanted to be able to be there with the others. But nothing in his life had yet set him up for being part of an organised group of strangers – the structure, amount of attention, concentration and compliance it required were impossible for him. He couldn't do it, so he flipped. He didn't mean to, he didn't really do it with the intention of making trouble.

That week was still a success, because it's about the young people being prepared even to go a step or two away from their comfort zone, and finding that it's not impossible, even if it doesn't go perfectly every time. The fact that they did eventually get out of the bus, they did register, they did take part in the week – they actually enjoyed it – that's an enormous success. Your expectations need to be pitched at a level that is realistic, and you need to be able to recognise and celebrate those small steps.

Niki's diary, 25 August 2005

I had my first success today. It was with Julie. She only started coming here because she was banned by another youth project. Everyone says she is quite difficult but I have been spending a bit of time with her over the past weeks and the stories people tell just don't fit with my experience of her. Since that funny thing about the collage, something seemed to change. That really put me off at first, but then I decided that I would not let it affect me, that I would try and love her anyway, and keep on just the same, whatever reaction I was getting.

She has this weird habit of patting people on the head. I mean, everyone, all the time, and she's sometimes quite rough, and definitely messes your hair up. She went to do it to me last week, and I wasn't having it, so I just said, 'You do <u>not</u> pat my head,' and she didn't speak to me for four days.

I thought that might be it, but then she let me back in. She came and sat next to me yesterday afternoon. She didn't pat me on the head, but once or twice, she just put her arm round me briefly. She's quite possessive in a way – she sort of guards the relationship she has with me I suppose. I hadn't even thought about it, but Sharon obviously noticed. She came up to me and said, 'You're getting on with Julie, aren't you? You seem to be doing something right.' It felt great. I mean, I haven't done anything dramatic with her at all. But over the months, I guess, something has slowly happened.

It takes a long time. I've been here four and a half months now. And this is my first personal positive success. Just a girl sitting down next to me wanting to talk to me.

8

Sex, Swearing and Stella Artois

Yan

A couple of years back, John took a few of the lads on a camping trip one weekend. Some of the group were Christians and others weren't. The two in the tent next to John had both recently started describing themselves as Christians. As he was going to bed, John heard some kind of argument break out between them. He could hear them tussling and having a go at each other. This was really annoying for John, because he was just ready to go to sleep, and now he was going to have to get up and sort it out. But as he listened, he realised what it was they're saying to each other:

'Oi, you ——, it's my turn to read the ——ing Bible! Give it here!

'No! —— you! I'm still looking at it.'

The lads' language would have been considered highly unbiblical by a lot of Christians, but the language wasn't really what John heard. He heard two lads arguing over whose turn it was to read the Word of God. That's major success! So John sighed with relief, smiled, lay back down on his mattress and left them to it.

We've completely got used to all sorts of language by now, but for a lot of people, to hear someone swearing immediately puts their Christianity into doubt. I've had that kind of reaction. Like, 'They can't possibly be Christians, using language like that.' But I would say two things to that. Firstly, that's massive cultural baggage that you're turning into a judgement on somebody's relationship with God, and secondly, if you really think swearing is the first and most important thing for somebody to get right, then where have you been all your life?

The big three are swearing, sex and drinking. That's what people get the most criticism for. But why should they be more crucial than other stuff? More than lustful thoughts, or fiddling your insurance claim, or being bitchy behind someone's back? I reckon Christians all over the place do those sorts of things all the time, but because they're not in your face, it doesn't seem to matter so much. Swearing and sex and drink are very obvious, so people seize on them, when actually I don't think they are the real issues.

Swearing is a cultural thing. So, for instance, in a certain culture I could say 'shit' and it would be very offensive. Say it here and no one bats an eyelid, because it doesn't mean anything. It's not surprising or shocking or unacceptable in any way. So Christians are imposing their own expectations and cultural frameworks on people from different cultural backgrounds. They are judging the kids according to rules that don't actually apply in the communities those kids belong to. It's like going to a foreign country and criticising the people there for not speaking very good English.

I don't come in on a Monday morning to a staff meeting and find that everyone goes quiet and looks at me reproachfully, and I go, 'Oh yes, sorry, I had a lustful thought on Friday night.' But if I came in and I had been drunk and yelling swear words on Friday night, then it's not necessarily better or worse, but it's just a lot more obvious – people would have seen and heard me, and there would definitely be a sense of outrage. At the end of the day, though, what is the difference? I genuinely don't know whether it's a cultural value or whether it's a Christian value not to swear. You can go to Scripture and find references to using your words carefully, cleansing your tongue, remembering how powerful words are, and not taking the name of the Lord in vain,[1] but none of that seems to actually be referring to swearing. And who's decided that any particular word is a swear word, and therefore wrong? Is there a list in the Bible – swear words of every age and language, broken down into how offensive they are and which ones you can and can't use in what circumstances? I've never found it. So we are confronted here with these sorts of things – suddenly you re-examine the values you grew up with and you constantly think, hang on, is that me or is that biblical?

Now yes, I happen to believe that in a perfect world, people wouldn't use bad language. But this world we're in is far from perfect, and it doesn't work like that anyway. Nobody becomes an angel overnight when they start to trust God. And I really think that God has better, more important plans for people than stopping them swearing.

I think when Niki arrived she was quite shocked by the swearing. And I have to say, it's not just the kids. It's also the staff. I think because she was so good, so Christian, I started noticing more that some of us on the staff swear a bit. I felt like it made her question what kind of Christians we were. The thing is, when you've been here a while, it kind of rubs off on you, but also – you stop judging people by what kinds of words they use, and because of that, you become less focused on using them yourself. I mean, that's not necessarily a good thing – but hopefully it means at least you are focused on what actually does matter.

John was taking a team from e:merge to a Christian football tournament once. It was being organised for a load of church teams from the area. This is when we were at the Vine still, so part of the church there. And John had done really well. He'd got the right number of lads for a team, he'd got them all up and out of bed, at the meeting place on time and in the right kit. He was proud of how professional they looked, and how punctual they were arriving at the ground where they were playing the tournament. They went all the way through the tournament without any incidents, and he was completely chuffed because they were really into it, and enjoying themselves, and none of them had tried to run away or started on anyone. It was a major triumph.

But at the end of the match, this guy came up to him, from one of the other teams, and said to John, 'You really should control your team better. They are using some foul language out there.'

Honestly! It's like someone climbs a mountain and you criticise them for burping at the top! For any of us who work with young people here, it's ridiculous – because we know how much it takes just for them to be there. And the fact that they haven't killed anyone or each other is fantastic!

You can see the funny side of it – you can say, 'Wow! I wish I could make that guy who had a go at me take on my football team for a while. I wish I could see how he would cope with it.' Yet at the same time, you can't just laugh it off, because it's actually quite depressing. It makes you feel isolated. I suppose it doesn't actually matter at the end of the day, because it's not that man who is ultimately going to judge whether we are doing good by these kids or not. But even so, imagine how good it would be if he actually understood what it was like for us. If he came up to John and instead of criticising him for something small like swearing, said, 'You've done a great job getting these kids here, and we're really glad they came and played football with us.' Imagine how great that would feel.

One big plus in all the football activities we do with the kids here is that we are always positive about them. We never have a go at them, we always praise them for what they do well and encourage them. And they're simply not used to that. They've often been told they are failures so we model Jesus to them, because Jesus believed in people, and saw their potential, and he encourages us to become what we can, rather than criticising us for not being there yet. And then you turn around and there's someone who's supposedly your brother in Christ getting completely the wrong end of the stick and judging you, and the kids, and not realising what a hard work it is you're engaged in.

Sometimes, I just want to turn around to someone and say, 'Right, you go and suffer ten years of abuse from your dad, you watch your mum get addicted to drugs, you spend your entire childhood bunking off school because all anyone tells you at school is how thick you are, you go through all that and then see if you can do it without swearing, drinking or having sex.' Thankfully, I resist, but it does scare me to think that many Christians in this country probably have a faith that doesn't resonate with this sort of area – with the very people that Jesus asks us to take care of.

Niki's diary, 5 September 2005

One of the parents came in today. She normally asks for Yan but instead she asked for <u>me</u> and talked to <u>me</u> about what she wanted to say. I was really surprised, and it was a bit of a breakthrough for me. I thought, oh they actually can see me, I'm the youth worker.

Also, I was talking to Julie during drop in today, and she said, 'Would you still talk to me if you knew I had stolen something?'

I replied, 'Well yes, Julie, I would. I would tell you I thought it was a bad idea to steal stuff, but I'd still talk to you.'

Then she was quiet for a bit before saying, 'If I told you I had stolen something, would you tell everyone else?'

'No of course not,' I said. Then I explained that I never talk about any of what the young people say to me, except in supervision, because that helps me deal with things in the best way – and then I always change the names and the details anyway. And the only other time is if someone's in danger I tell Sharon because she's the child protection officer, and we follow the guidelines for that, for their safety. She nodded but didn't say anything else. I said, 'Have you stolen something, Julie?' and she shook her head.

'No. I'm just working you out. I'm working out what you're really like.' Then she suddenly said, 'I think you can be trusted,' but as soon as she'd said it, she walked away.

Yan

John went to the house of one of the young lads one day, to talk to his dad about a trip this lad wanted to go on. After they'd had their discussion, the little brother of the lad – who was about eight years old – wanted to show John his football sticker book, because it was nearly complete. So John follows the boy into the next room where there's a big pile of papers and magazines. The boy starts picking up all these porn magazines from off the top of the pile, sorting through them to find his sticker book. John couldn't believe it, but the boy was completely unfazed. He saw John's face, and just went, 'Yeah, my dad's a dirty bugger,' and finally found his sticker book, half way down the pile.

Another time, John was doing a session on sex with some of the lads, and in the context of influences and role models, they were talking about when they first learnt about sex and who they learnt it from. One of the kids, only about eleven or twelve, said 'from watching porn with my Dad'. From the way he told it, it seemed his dad kind of said, 'Right, you're old enough now son,' reached for the remote and said, 'check this out, this is what happens.'

Another lad, about the same age, said, 'From watching my mum and her boyfriend when they come back from the pub, on the couch in the front room.'

Frank is a really strong lad we have worked with for some years, who is now in his early twenties. He has committed himself to God and is on a real faith journey. Now that he is older than most of our young people here he wants to move on from relying on e:merge for his spiritual input but he finds it hard. Reading and concentrating on his own are difficult for him, and yet when he goes to church, he doesn't understand the sermons particularly well, and he feels as though everyone else is different from him – as though he is on the periphery.

He also finds the relationships situation very difficult. All his contemporaries and his friends are in relationships with the opposite sex, and enjoying sexual activity. He has been taught – and he understands – that God wants us to save sexual activity for marriage. He wants to get married. He wants to fall in love, start a family, but he comes into contact with very few women who share faith like his. He would like to go to camps like Soul Survivor and meet more Christians his age, but there's no way he can afford to go. So what is he to do? He recently started seeing a young woman from the area who did not have a Christian faith, and he received very quick criticism from Christian friends about it, telling him to stop the relationship straight away. I was really disappointed to hear that, because he was hurt by the way they were quick to jump in and tell him what he should not be doing, and yet did not engage with him to find other solutions to his situation.

I agree with him that the best way for us to live is within marital relationships, but when he can't find that marital relationship, I personally find it very hard to tell him that he must not go out with non-Christians. I do believe that God wants us to save sex for marriage, but that's because in his desire for our well-being, he wants us to be in caring, positive, permanent relationships. It's not because he fundamentally does not want us to have sex! It's all got muddled. It started off as a healthy way of living that would honour God, and it ends up as being a list of dos and don'ts that we have tacked on to God's supposedly unconditional love for us.

The fact is, Frank is strong in his faith, but struggling to belong. And the church, in its intransigent focus on a few particular aspects of lifestyle, often makes it harder for him to belong rather than easier.

Niki's diary, 9 September 2005

The young people here are not sophisticated in their language and expressing themselves. Quite a few times, someone has come to me in a bit of a state, confused, not understanding what's going on in their own heads. They will find themself in a crisis, and they'll say, 'Help me understand what I'm thinking!' So they definitely don't think about what the most appropriate ways are to address God. Once, in Xstream, we were talking about families and praying for our families. Yan had asked if we could pray for his brother because he needed a car. And this young guy, I think it was probably his first prayer, just prayed, 'Dear God, give Yan's brother a car or else I'm going to come and batter you!'

The cell leader at that time was a young lad called Darren, and after that session Yan must have said something to him like, 'You handle their prayers really well, you're doing really well,' as an encouragement. But Darren replied, 'Oh, that was nothing. Last time we had cell, we were doing prayers for things we were thankful to God for, and Carl prayed, 'Thank you God that I have the biggest cock in my class!'

Sometimes, you don't quite know whether they're doing it to wind you up, or whether it's genuine. There's nothing you can say to something like that – you just let it happen. But the main thing is, some of these prayers are their first moments with God, their first interaction. I think some Christians would be like, 'Oh you can't pray that! You can't say <u>that</u>.' But I think God's probably more likely to be thinking, 'Wow, this person's just made a step towards me. This young person who has known nothing but trouble and rebellion all their lives has just spoken to me for the first time.' God's big enough to cover his ears for the swear words. I just don't think it offends him. I think he's bigger than that.

Yan

I think God is generous. I think God wants us to get it right. He's not waiting for these kids to fail, he's longing for them to succeed. I really think he rejoices at whatever movement anyone makes towards him. I think he can hack all sorts of things going wrong if that overall movement towards him is there.

We often find that a lot of the journey these kids take is very up and down. They'll become a Christian and at first it's great, and then their lifestyle will kind of go to pot a bit and they'll come back and go, 'Let's get sorted,' but then it'll go to pot again and they'll come back, and so on. There's a lot of that yo-yoing, but all the time, the challenge for us is to keep our patience. We try and be accepting – to say, 'It's OK. We're just working it out. God still loves you.' I think the worst thing you can do is to come in and go, 'That thing you're doing in your life, well that's completely wrong and you have to sort it out right now.' Rubbish. They're in a relationship with God and that relationship will have its ups and downs – just like any other relationship in life, strong one day, weak the next. And that's OK. We all have so much stuff to work through, however long we have been Christians. It's just that with most people, it's more hidden, subtle things like attitudes, the way we use money, putting our security in the wrong places. Our 'stuff' is just less obvious. We have Christian kids that come in with a black eye or something, and when we ask what happened they sort of hang their heads and say, 'I got drunk on Friday night and ended up battering this lad in the toilets.' They don't need us to point out that that wasn't a clever thing to do. They need us to go, 'God still loves you, and you can still change.'

The fact is, we don't realise how much we have let our culture affect our theology. The reason Christians make a big deal about smoking, for example, is not because Jesus talks a lot about smoking in the Bible. He doesn't. The reason they make a big deal about it is that it's part of their traditional ethos and cultural expectation that good people don't smoke, and somewhere along the line, this has got mixed up with their theology and become, 'People who smoke are not Christians.' I don't think anyone would argue with the fact that smoking is unhealthy and not a good way to treat your body – but being a non-smoker is not part of the essence of Christianity.

So what working in this place has done for me, and I see this happening to all the staff here, too, is forced me to re-examine my faith. It has made me strip it down and ask what part of it is really real? How much of my faith is what has been built up around me, and how much is actually from God?

When you read the Bible again after being in this environment, you find that the stuff we thought was all nice and neatly defined in black and white lines actually isn't. You look at it with new eyes, and you see that we've written those lines in because we are uncomfortable with any degree of uncertainty. If you sit down and ask most Christians, where in the Bible does it say, for example, that you can't have sex before you're married, they won't know. And yet this lack of understanding does not prevent them placing strict expectations on other people's lives and sexual behaviour.

Here at e:merge, we have to challenge our faith every day. We don't have a choice. We have to shake ourselves up, and if we don't do it ourselves, then our faith gets shaken up for us by the people we see here, the way things are. So you're constantly re-examining your beliefs and that's scary. Because when you move out of the black and white, you're moving outside of your security. You go through a transition where all the things you thought were true and important are all of a sudden being challenged and rocked. Some of them you hold on to, and some of them you leave behind. Then you get to another place of faith, you get rid of some beliefs and you shape the ones that you're holding on to.

What that does, though, in the end, is make your faith more solid. When everything that can be shaken has been shaken, you're left with the unshakeable. Which is a pretty good foundation.

I arrived here like Niki, thinking things were black and white. But you can't survive here and still maintain that it's all black and white. This kind of place is a living contradiction to some of the ideas we traditionally have about Christianity. You can't make sense of them both at once. You realise that it's not stark black and white. There is a whole lot of grey. But what you learn is, God is in the grey.

Niki's diary, 23 September 2005

I spent some time with Julie this afternoon before Xstream. She seemed like she wanted to chat, so I asked her if she wanted to go for a walk and she agreed. We just talked about nothing for a while, then she started telling me about her home situation. Her dad died about a year ago, and then her uncle moved in with her and her mum. Her uncle is beating her up. She showed me bruises, up high on her arm where they are covered by her T shirt. I couldn't believe it. She explained that she couldn't tell her mum because it's her mum's brother – he gives them money and her mum keeps saying, 'I don't know what I'd do without uncle so and so around.' She tries to keep out of the house when her mum's not there because that's when it happens – but staying out is not always possible.

I said, 'Julie, thank you for telling me this – I am really glad you felt you could tell me.' She told me very insistently that she didn't want the police contacted, and I have to respect this. I said, 'Whenever you need to talk, just let me know, and if you want to text, you can text me day or night,' but beyond that, what could I say? I wanted to say, 'God will get you out of this situation,' but what do I know? It's a person's life and you can't promise things like that when you don't actually know what will happen. I felt privileged that she had opened up to me, and at the same time, I felt like I was already letting her down, for not being able to instantly get her out of that situation. I am asking God for wisdom for me and safety for her.

Note

[1] E.g. James 3:1–12, Psalm 19:14, Exodus 20:7.

9

We Came, We Saw, We Converted

Yan

When I first arrived here, telling people about Jesus was everything to me. I wanted to see this whole area transformed and turned to God. I set out to tell the good news to as many people as I could, as quickly as possible.

One day, when I was still quite new in the area, I was sitting on a park bench talking to a woman who worked in a local community centre. I had got to know her a little, as I went to her centre to keep contact with the young people there. It was not a Christian place, and she wasn't a Christian, but she knew that I was. As we sat on the bench there, she suddenly asked me, 'So, I'm going to hell then, am I?' It was a bit of a blunt question that I wasn't prepared for, so I kind of ignored her at first, and pretended I hadn't heard. But she kept on. 'Come on, I want to know. Where do I stand?' So I said to her, 'Well, if you don't know Jesus then of course you're going to hell.'

When I think about that, I cringe. I would never be so blunt now. In fact, I wouldn't be so sure about it theologically now, let alone actually tell someone that to her face. But back then she took me by surprise and I responded with all I knew to say. She argued with me for a few minutes and then just got up and walked away. I felt pretty stupid because I didn't know what to do after that. I felt like I'd been tricked by the question, but also I realised that I should have had a much more rounded response.

Some fundamental things have changed for me over these twelve years. I've become less interested in whether the people I'm working with become Christians or not. People may think that's really controversial, but it's the reality of where I'm at in my personal journey. I think Christ has called us to make a difference in our world. There will always be people who accept him and there will always be others who do not. We work with both. Even the ones who do not accept him, we will continue to serve and love and help them progress in their lives. I don't think Jesus stopped relating to people who didn't choose him at the first opportunity.

When we speak to churches or church organisations, we will often get the question, 'How many young people have become Christians through your work?' That question really frustrates us. When Christians talk purely in terms of conversions it's like they are reducing people to commodities – as though the beginning and end of our work is this particular moment when young people turn to faith in Christ. There is so much more to it than that.

My ideal for this project would not be that every young person involved in it becomes a Christian. My ideal for this project would be that every young person involved in it becomes a Christian, avoids becoming ensnared in addiction, is released and healed from past hurts and family conflicts, becomes skilled, secures appropriate housing, has a job they can enjoy and in which they can progress, builds healthy, lasting relationships and enlarges their horizons so they can have confidence in tackling any kind of challenge life might bring. I'm interested in their entire lives, not just in whether they tick my faith box.

I am convinced that Jesus is the answer. I believe that the way to God is through Christ. I believe that once somebody comes to know Christ and has a relationship with God, they are complete. But what has changed for me is the belief that, even outside of that experience of becoming a Christian, Christ still wants people to be more complete, he still wants people to become more like who he's made them to be – to fulfil their potential. Even if they don't end up believing in him. For a young person who's come through our programmes and who hasn't accepted Christ, God's desire is still for that person to be all that they can be. I don't think God stops working, or expects us to – he can still build all sorts of amazing things into that young person. Yes, eternal salvation might be lost to that person. Yes, some of the amazing benefits in this world of believing in Christ will be lost to that person, but I think in God's mercy somehow he continues to build into those young people the goodness that he is and that he brings. I think God wants people to do well in life, whether or not they decide to follow him.

So if young people do arrive at their own faith in Christ, that is something we are very excited about. But if they choose not to believe in him, that's fine as well. At the end of the day, we have taken up the 'Great Commission' (Matthew 28:16–20) and we are preaching the gospel to the young people in this area. Whether they accept Christ or not is up to them, and the Holy

Spirit. Our job is to tell them, and then to keep loving them whatever they choose.

It sounds really obvious when you write it down here, but it's amazing how many churches or Christian people seem only to be interested in others because they might become Christians. Our relationship with our young people is never like that. Never. Whether they become a Christian quickly, slowly or never at all, that relationship's still there. Our friendship isn't contingent on them finding faith. It's not contingent on them finding a job, or even them joining in with the stuff we do or whatever. We have to 'be Jesus' to these young people, and I don't think Jesus walked away from people just because they didn't immediately agree with everything he said.

It's absolutely brilliant when a young person here becomes a Christian. It's also brilliant when a young person grows in self-confidence and starts relating to other people in a more wholesome way. If a young person gets a job that's a big celebration. Instead of living on the dole, now suddenly there's an opportunity for him or her to move on and make something out of their lives and deal with some of the issues that deprivation and poverty have saddled them with. Surely that's a gift of God to that young person?

Too often we see spiritual salvation as a sort of ticket out of the mess of this world, but actually, God's salvation is as much about equipping us to deal with the reality of life on this earth as it is about making us ready for the new heaven and new earth beyond. Once we grasp this, we will see that God has an interest in the whole person, the whole way through their life.

Niki's diary, 29 September 2005

I've discovered that the kids love baking. Not just the girls, the boys, too. I made some biscuits with them the other day, and they loved it. They love the idea of making something and then eating it as well. I kind of thought they might think it was childish or girlie, but they thought it was well cool, and yesterday when they came to drop in, about four of them kept going, 'Can we do some baking Niki? Please, can we?' It's not easy because you need to have enough staff cover to take a group of them into the kitchen and for everyone to be properly supervised, but there's something really nice about the joy they had about it.

When we did the baking the other day, we thought we might have run out of oil at one stage for greasing the trays, and I went, 'Where's Elisha when you need him!' thinking of the miracle of the oil in the Old Testament (2 Kings 4). The kids just looked at me blankly and asked, 'Who's Elisha?' I started explaining about the widow and the miracle and the prophet – but they lost track. Jonny asked, 'What's a testament?' and I thought, it's going to take me half an hour to explain my six word comment, and by then the cakes will be burnt anyway! So I said, 'Oh, it doesn't matter,' and kept stirring the mixture. Jonny shook his head and went, 'Niki, you're such a nutter.'

Yan

This is the other point about people asking what our conversion tally is – you have to remember just how little people here know about Jesus. That's one of the things that really amazed Sharon and me when we arrived. In the early days, before we had a youth congregation, Sharon had taken a couple of the young people to church. There were two fifteen-year-olds with us – Jake and Ashley. Ashley was sitting next to Sharon and the minister was speaking at the front of the church. He had been speaking for some time, mostly about heaven, revival and things like that. The two lads were sat quite quietly and seemed to be listening. Then the minister mentioned something about Judgement Day, and Ashley just went, '*Now* I know what he's talking about!' Sharon kind of looked at him and he looked at her as though everything had suddenly become very obvious, and he said, 'Terminator Two!'

'What do you mean "Terminator Two"?' Sharon asked.

'*Terminator Two! The Judgement Day!* He's talking about the film!'

And Sharon realised that everything the minister had been saying for the last half hour had had no frame of reference for Ashley in Ashley's world. So suddenly, he had latched on to the first reference point that he could find and that was the Arnold Schwarzenegger film *Terminator Two*, because its subtitle is *Judgement Day*. Up until that point, it had all been complete gobbledegook for him, and now he seriously thought the minister was standing up at the front of church giving a whole talk about an action film.

That was the point where Sharon and I realised that we couldn't presume any knowledge at all about Jesus or Christianity. We realised we'd have to assume that everything we said to the young people about God or the Bible was cryptic – we would really have to go back to the basics, breaking everything down piece by piece.

At Easter time that same year, Sharon and I did a discussion evening with the youth. We must have had about thirty to thirty-five young people in the room. We were discussing what happened at Easter and we got to the resurrection and we explained how we believed that Jesus had risen from the dead, and one young lad just said to us, 'Get out of town! That did not happen. I have *never* heard that before.'

Sharon asked him, 'You've never heard about Jesus being raised from the dead?'

'Never. When did that happen?'

We explained how after Jesus died, his empty tomb was found with the stone rolled away, and how Jesus had then appeared to quite a lot of people, and finally his friends had seen him taken up to heaven. We explained how we believed that God had raised Jesus from the dead, and that showed how he was stronger than everything – even death. The lad had heard about Jesus dying, but never that Jesus had been raised from the dead. So I asked, out of interest, how many of the group had never heard of Jesus being raised from the dead – more than half of them. Some knew he'd died on the cross but didn't know anything about the resurrection.

John had the same thing. He was in a cell group with kids who were doing an Xposure course, which is when they are taught the basics of the gospel. He'd only been here a few months and was running through some discussion-sparking stuff like, if Jesus were born today, what would he look like? What would he wear? The young people were saying things like, he would drive a motorbike and wear a leather jacket and things like that. Then they started to get confused.

John had just said, '. . . and Jesus lived in Nazareth, which is in Israel.'

One lad suddenly frowned and said, 'I don't get it,' turning to John he asked, 'So how long has he been here, then?'

'What?' said John.

'How long has Jesus been here – like, how long has he been touring?'

It turned out the lad literally thought Jesus was a rock star – that he'd just arrived to do the UK leg of a tour, and that's why we were all suddenly talking about him.

And people expect us to have mass, fast conversions in this kind of context? Even when Jesus came to earth, the Jews all knew who God was – they knew the stories about Abraham and Isaac and Jacob, and how they were God's people, and God would one day come and rescue them by sending a Messiah or chosen one to save them. So even if they didn't agree with or believe in Jesus, at least they had common cultural currency to understand him with. We don't have that here any more.

We all want to tell these young people about God but we do it by building stepping stones that are close enough for them to manage.

They know we are a Christian project, but we don't start by preaching at them – we start by meeting them where they are and welcoming them. We go out on detached work, so the kids know we are prepared to come to them – we are not afraid to be on the streets, in the places where they hang out. From there, we invite them into the drop-in, which is a few times a week in the e:merge building. Many young people find that approachable enough to come to, but even a drop-in session can be intimidating for some, so we don't push it. Some will get to know me for a long time on the streets, seeing me around and sussing me out for a year or so even, before coming to a drop-in session.

We never hide our Christianity, but we don't ram it down anyone's throat either. The drop-ins we run express the fact that we are interested in all aspects of their lives, not just preaching at them. There are computers where they can job search, do homework, print things out from the web and play games. There are pool tables. They can make cups of tea. We do arts and crafts for those that are into creative things. We do some football sessions, some exercise sessions or aerobics, we have little talks or demonstrations about, say, healthy eating or interview skills. We hardly ever have any specific 'God spot' or planned faith-based input to the drop-ins, because that isn't what we've invited the young people to – it would be like getting them in under false pretences. We are always there if they have questions about God, but at drop-in we generally only talk about our beliefs if the conversation is initiated by a young person.

People will talk about certain activities having 'Christian content' and what they actually mean is content that tries to induce the person experiencing it to make a commitment to God. Our content includes welcoming people, providing for their practical needs, being available to help with emotional needs and enabling them to build positive relationships with each other. How can that possibly not be 'Christian'? Christian worship is about everything that we do, and honouring God in the whole of our lives – whether in a church, on the street, at home or anywhere. So our belief in Jesus is just as inherent in our drop-in sessions or at the Academy as in our Xposure course and the organised worship we have on Friday nights – Xstream.

We always long for young people to experience Christ, to learn more about him, but we don't force them to come to the more obviously teaching-focused elements of our work. They will come when they want to. Often it means a period of months or even years for them to get comfortable with us and with the project. They observe how we live our lives, and take time to trust that we have their welfare at heart. They will perhaps get involved in sports sessions or something similar, and start to know some of the other young people and feel part of the crowd. Then perhaps at a certain point, they start wanting to know more about the beliefs that they know motivate us.

They might come to Xstream on a Friday night and sit, watch and listen. For the first time they are in a congregation hearing about Jesus and seeing their peers focusing on God together. God created us, and he knows more intimately than anyone else the nature of our very being. So when we enter into relationship with God, through Jesus, we start to get to know our creator and that is the ultimate opportunity to know ourselves. That's part of introducing young people to faith – the opportunity to really know and understand themselves, to become something more true to what they were created for.

It's really exciting to see that, but I think one of the things that makes it possible for young people to turn up and feel safe about it is that they know we work with them equally in the different areas – practical, emotional, educational and spiritual. We're not running everything else as a kind of funnel into our more overtly faith-based events. It all makes a whole. We believe strongly that everyone has spiritual needs, but also, God's concept of salvation is to meet all of our needs, to satisfy every part of us. If you separate off the need for spiritual salvation from the need to be fulfilled in every other part of life, too, you deny the holistic reality of God and the very sense of what it is to be a complete human being. God did not make us just spirits, or just bodies, he made us people, and he wants us to be whole people.

We hold Xstream here in the large hall, and it's our way of trying to make organised worship and teaching accessible for young people who probably do not experience it elsewhere. It's just one of the ways that young people who have – or are journeying towards – a faith can express themselves with God and each other. We usually have some singing and a very short, simple talk about God. Then we break down into cell groups, many of which are led by peer leaders rather than youth workers. In cell groups, we normally discuss what the talk has been about, and try and get young people to look at their own lives and how what was said might be relevant to them. Sometimes they will pray, if there's an appetite for that, and everything we do we try and do in an interactive, accessible way. We don't hit them with a load of heavy theology. We very much talk about the nature of God, the character of God, and then the ideas of salvation and forgiveness, so young people really can learn about what Christianity believes and stands for. If they want to make their own commitment, then they can do that at their own pace.

We get a real range of people at Xstream. Quite a few of our young people come from church backgrounds. They have come from Christian families and have had their own faith, sometimes for many years. We are so grateful to God for those young people who have been faithful for a long time. They make for a really solid foundation for others to draw strength from. Then we have others who have recently come to a faith in Jesus, from a background of never having attended church, and their parents and grandparents never having attended church. Still others are there out of interest, or because they have started their own journey, but have not yet decided whether they want to follow Jesus or not. We try and make it as broad as possible in the welcome, because it's a wonderful opportunity to introduce young people to God. Again, it's low pressure. There's no sense of going, 'Hey that young person has been coming to Xstream for four months, they should be making a commitment by now.' It's all about building people's knowledge of God so that they can make decisions themselves, in the long term, in the context of their own lives. You can't tell them they have to behave a certain way, or live up to a certain standard before they're welcome, and you can't put a time limit on anyone. You just have to keep putting your little pinches of salt in, and if a young person wants to go further, they will in their own time, and we accept that.

Also, you can't specify the process or the way in which people start coming. We had one lad turn up at Xstream once because he wanted to find another lad he had a grudge against and beat him up. The guy he wanted to beat up wasn't there, but he discovered he liked Xstream, so he kept on coming!

Our programmes are designed to expose young people to God and to explore faith in a real way. Yes, I believe that they need Jesus. But what they need is the real Jesus, not the Jesus who we use to chalk them up as a conversion on our church's blackboard. Not the interpretation that we have put on Jesus from our backgrounds and experiences. Not a Jesus who says, conform to this, look like that, behave like the other, and then – if you're lucky – we'll condescend to consider you a Christian. No way. They need the Jesus who says, 'Just as you are, that's all right. Come on a journey with me.'

Another option for young people who want to find out more about God is the course we offer called Xposure, which explains the basics of the gospel. It's a 24-hour residential experience where we go through who Jesus is, why he died for us and why we need him. We encourage anyone who shows an interest in understanding more about God to come along.

We run Xposure a few times a year. We wrote it ourselves because trying to find anything resource-wise that these kids would identify with, that fits their experience of the world, was very difficult. It's just a very simple way of presenting the gospel. For example, we will start by drawing a line of good and bad. We say, 'This end is 100 per cent good, and that end is 100 per cent bad. Where are you on the line?' We get some photos of celebrities – where are these people? Then we ask, 'Where on the line do you think God's standard is? That's God's standard up there at 100 per cent good, miles away from where you've put yourself and I've put myself – so what are we going to do about this difference? Well, what Jesus came to do was make up that difference.' That's how we start explaining it. We don't use the words sin and forgiveness until they understand what we're talking about. We go as far back to the basics as necessary, and we try and give each person the time they need for things to sink in. Doing things simply, in small chunks, and often repeating key messages and leaving enough time for them to understand is vital. Otherwise you're not getting your message across.

Those of our young people who are searching for God have experiences of the Holy Spirit, where they feel

God's presence in a very real way. That is wonderful because they are encouraged and inspired, they know something has happened, and it builds their faith. However, there is a danger present if you don't get the balance right between experiences and knowledge. We are aware of the need not to make young people's experience of God a solely emotional one. In this environment where it takes young people a long time to learn and understand facts, concepts and ideas, it could be easy to lean too heavily on their emotional experiences of God. It is completely wonderful when the Holy Spirit is present, and young people have an experience of him. That is something that can happen any time, anywhere, and no matter how little they have learnt about Christianity or God. However, we do make sure that we always supplement their experiences with teaching and theology, because otherwise they may rely solely on the warm feelings and the heart relationship rather than a head relationship as well. Given how low the bar is of existing knowledge, and the time it can take for explanations and concepts to sink in with young people who are not used to learning, it is really important to be prepared to take time over this.

Being aware of the potential for emotionalism is important because otherwise, you are allowing an environment to develop where people could potentially be abused – by following a particularly charismatic leader, or by buying in to an emotional group experience without being able to analyse and sift that experience for themselves. We don't want young people to become Christians because they had a warm, fuzzy feeling on a Friday night. We want them to make a decision because the warm, fuzzy feeling has been coupled with rational explanations of belief that they have tested for themselves and decided to live by.

So in this, we find a real challenge. We must reach out to a culture where it is not always cool to learn, and find ways to connect with young people who have no relationship with traditional methods of learning and communication. However, once we have made a connection with them, it is no use leaving them where they are. We want them to learn. We don't want them to rely on us for their input. We would rather they are taught to seek and find knowledge themselves. We want to make disciples, not one-off conversions. We try to walk alongside those who are seeking, so that we can build theological understanding into them. In their place of heart-knowledge, we teach them to desire head knowledge so they can make rational decisions and wise judgements. We are not content with their low levels of literacy, just as they are not. We have to reach them in a way that is not reliant on the written word, but we don't want to ignore the importance of the word either. So once we have a connection and they have a desire for God, we will help them learn to read the Bible for themselves. We will encourage them to do this, but we can only do it once we have arrived where they're at – we can't do it from far away.

Niki's diary, 3 October 2005

One of the things that's different around here is, it's not 'come in, preach the message, go home', it's 'come in, make the place your home, then live the message'. That's what Yan and Sharon are doing. It's a whole lot harder than a summer evangelism campaign or a beach mission or something. It also requires a whole lot more commitment. But it's more holistic, more lasting.

I have really wanted to talk more to Julie about her situation but since I had that chat with her, she has kept hanging out with me at dop in and stuff, but has completely avoided being on her own with me. I think she must feel so vulnerable having finally told someone about the situation. I am trying to be patient, just letting her do it all at her own pace, but I am finding it so hard.

This month's 'Youthwork' magazine arrived today. I turned straight to the jobs page again before I even thought about it. I hope no one noticed.

Yan

I think the biggest thing for us is that any young person who comes in here is given a positive picture of Christ. So if they never make a decision for God, we're not going to judge them for that. We're not going to make them feel that they've failed us in some way because they haven't opted for a relationship with God. We know at some time God will use the experiences they've had with us, and the words they've heard from us, and we want them to be open to the next time God puts something into their lives. The last thing we want is for next time, someone to react negatively saying, 'I didn't opt for Christianity last time and those people who talked to me about God didn't want anything to do with me any more.' That would be awful, and the worst testimony you could possibly give.

We want people to know God's love. We don't want our evangelism to be pressured, because we don't believe that's what God wants. If God wants to force people to become Christians quickly, he is very capable of doing that – but more often I think he gives us reasons and understanding and experiences that together lead us to him. He puts people in our lives who can explain and model Jesus to us. He does this surely and thoroughly – not necessarily quickly.

Say we work with a particular young person who does not make a decision for Christ while we are working with them. In Christian terms, e:merge may not reap that fruit – but somebody else might. As long as when that young person leaves us, whatever they've heard about God is positive, whatever they have experienced of us as people is honest and caring, it doesn't matter. Our understanding of the kingdom of God is not that every young person who comes through our doors needs to 'become a Christian'. It's much broader than that. It's that we are partners with many people across this area, this country, this world, all working for God and for people. God is sovereign, we get to play a small part, and his plans are more enormous than we could fathom. We play our role at a certain time, and from then on it's up to the Holy Spirit. We leave it in his hands.

I know that some people could judge from the outside and say that what we do is not 'Christian enough', it's not evangelistic enough, it's not challenging enough. I think that God's love in its own right is challenging. For young people who really, seriously doubt the fact that anybody loves them, to then learn about God loving them unconditionally is enormously challenging – to be told that although they have made bad choices and their life is in a mess, God loves them the same amount that he loves someone who has never done anything 'really bad', is beyond their understanding. They've never known anything like it before.

We haven't come to give the last little push to someone who has nearly enough faith to believe in Jesus. We have come to people who have no faith at all. Who have no knowledge, no wisdom, no hope.

The hope of God is that Jesus came as fully human. So everything Jesus was, we can be. All of us. Not just some, not just the ones who can read well, or are articulate or who did well at sports. Everyone. Faith is a journey towards the fullness of Christ, being transformed into his likeness. What we are doing is joining young people on that journey, and where they want us to, we help them travel that journey, from wherever they are now to wherever they might get to next, by the grace of God.

What's also important is that we don't have a hidden agenda. We don't relate to them, show them friendship only for the sake of trying to make them become Christians. We relate to them and show them friendship for friendship's sake and for their sake. Because they are young people. We don't need any other reason. Equally, we don't pretend that we're not about Christianity. We are open to them, so they can see that we're not suddenly trying to spring something on them. We're honest about it, and whatever else happens, they respect that.

That was the case in the end with the woman on the park bench after I'd told her she was going to hell. I had to work hard to keep that relationship after making such a comment, no question about it. But I think because I'm an open person, because at least I was being honest in responding to her question, and because she could see that I hadn't stopped talking to her because of her potentially going to hell, we did maintain a relationship in the end.

It's also because she has seen that I'm still here. She has seen me grow up, mature in a way. I didn't just turn up, preach then leave. She's seen me stick around, even after I have made a fool of myself. We have been able to rebuild that relationship, not because she now believes in Christ, but because she sees that I am still interested in her – and in the young people – whatever their response to Christianity.

I'd say we're good friends now, and we do talk from time to time about God and about spiritual issues – and the fact that we do actually derives from that original incident. So even though I put my foot in it, it wasn't altogether negative in the end. But she never lets me forget it. Every so often, in the middle of a discussion we're having, she'll suddenly smile and say, 'But don't listen to anything I say – I'm going to hell, remember?'

10

The Magic Prayer

Yan

Sometimes I wonder how many more things there are in my life and my faith that I am going to need to totally rediscover before God is through with me. As soon as you've realised that your work is all about loving people, and less about ticking off how many become Christians, you suddenly ask yourself, hang on a minute, how do I know when someone has become a Christian anyway?

If someone asks us how many young people in our project have become Christians, how do we answer that? OK, there are a few obvious ones – young people who have made a public commitment, who have actually said, 'I'm a Christian now,' but what about the ones who we know have started a journey, but who don't yet have everything sussed out to make a personal commitment. What about the ones who heard the gospel here, but had to go through another two projects, meet another seven Christian friends, before they then made a commitment years later? Do we count them? And what about all the people who are much closer to God now than they ever were, and perhaps pray, but don't yet count themselves as Christians?

What does it mean to become a Christian? Am I going to measure it at the point at which someone says the 'prayer of salvation', and we respond and say 'Right, that's that, now you are a Christian'? What does that mean somewhere like this? And anyway, is it up to me to know or to decide when someone has become a Christian? Whichever way you count it, the answer ends up being meaningless.

Our concept of salvation – our definition of what makes someone 'become a Christian' – is so influenced by our social expectations, the history of how we have behaved in our particular world. Within mainstream, evangelical Christianity, it tends to be, 'Come to the front, say the prayer, and hey presto! Now you're saved!' and someone tells you you're a Christian, and you move on – which means, by the way, that from now on you don't steal cars and you go to church regularly and you sit still and quietly, and you behave and you don't spit on the steps or stick your chewing gum to the chairs and so on and so on. Is that what it's about?

Jesus just loved talking to people and healing them. He didn't say, 'Right, you've become my follower, now you're going to be like this and this and this.' He did often say to people, 'Stop sinning,' but only *after* he'd touched them, healed them or transformed their life. Only when they themselves already knew they had sin in their life that they wanted to be free from.

People loved listening to Jesus. The Bible shows that crowds of people gathered wherever he went. But if anything, Jesus made it difficult for people to follow him, in the sense of committing their lives. He said it was a hard decision. This kind of life won't necessarily be easy, so sit down and think about it (see Luke 14:28–33). And instead of *telling* people what they believed, He asked them. He *asked* the disciples, 'Who do you say I am?' That was the point at which they could state that they'd had a revelation of him as the Messiah. 'You are the Christ, the Son of the living God,' said Peter. It started with Peter voicing his own revelation – and that's when Jesus responded, 'Yes, and I'm going to use you, Peter, to build my church' (see Matthew 16:13–20, author's own words).

We're not going to count, such-and-such number of young people came forward at the meeting and 'said the prayer' to give their lives to God. We definitely resist categorising people and trying to measure success in that way. All the time, we encourage young people to pray, to express themselves to God, but we look at faith as being a journey. Every step that a young person takes on that journey closer to the reality of Jesus Christ and having the reality of Jesus Christ in their life is a blessing.

There are some really basic beliefs that Christians have about what defines a 'Christian', which actually are as much to do with culture than they are to do with Jesus. So, the Christianity we have been used to previously might say, the true mark of someone who is spiritual is that you have your quiet time every day, where you pray and read your Bible. There's nothing wrong with that. In fact, there's a lot that's very right about that. But imagine you live with four other children, that you share a bedroom, that your mum or dad is ill and requires care, that someone in your family is alcoholic, or that you are hiding from an abusive partner. Perhaps your dad or older brother is in prison, and your mum works all the hours of the day at a low-paid job and you care for your siblings. Imagine you are afraid of someone in your household, or they are using the house to take drugs, so you spend as much of your time as possible on the streets rather than at home. Or imagine that you can't read very well, and trying to read anything makes you feel inadequate, stupid and frustrated. How do you do your quiet time then?

Bradford's literacy levels are a good deal lower than the average across England. The city has the highest level of people with no qualifications in West Yorkshire – and that is already higher than the national average.[1] It's so easy to place expectations on people that actually depress their faith journey, rather than lifting them up and encouraging them. It's so easy to think that your expectations are Bible-based, just because they've been drummed into you for so long, when actually they are cultural. Where does the Bible say, 'Have a quiet time of prayer and Bible-reading every day, preferably at the beginning of the day?' It doesn't. There are a lot of times where Jesus went off by himself and prayed in the desert all night. Do most Christians I know do that? When God told Joshua to meditate on the Book of the Law day and night – was he expecting Joshua to carry his pocket-sized NIV everywhere he went? What about before the printing press was invented? Did Christians have personal Bible reading times then? Clearly not. Were they real Christians then?

If we stop and we are daring enough to question ourselves, we will sometimes find that a frightening number of the truths we thought were straight out of the Bible are in fact more to do with our church background. What are we doing imposing those things on other people?

We encourage young people to enrich their relationship with God in ways that are relevant and helpful to them. For many, it is easier to pray with

a friend than alone. It is easier to listen to somebody
explain the Bible to you than read it for yourself. The
overall thing is to be searching after God. I think in
our Western, educated culture, we sometimes make
the Christian walk too individualistic. Yes, some things
are just between me and God, but actually, many of
the aspects of my faith are very much about relating
to other people as I worship, learn and work. Look at
the Trinity – God the Father, Son and Holy Spirit in
mutual interdependence. God himself is a community.
Surely that must suggest something to us about the
way we live. Why have we focused so much on the
silent, personal aspects of relating to him?

Here you find very much that faith is a journey, just
like life is, and that's the reality. It's a journey – and the
more people there are walking with you and around
you, the better you will travel. 'Saying the prayer' here
is mostly irrelevant. OK, there are some cases where
that is a good trigger, and does enable a young person
who is in the right space and has already been doing
a lot of thinking, to make their personal decision. But
what is really important is that people start walking
the journey. They will fall back many, many times, and
so you might have to repeat the same prayer over and
over. And often their falling back is more dramatic than
yours or mine, because the place they have started from
is so different and it's so much more difficult to climb
up that path again. But the point is, they are on the
path still. When you read the Psalms, David was just
the same – making huge mistakes, falling back in his
walk with God, stumbling, getting back up, repeating
the same prayers over and over, because nothing
seemed to be getting sorted.

Sharon was doing an all-girl cell group once and
asked for somebody to pray. One girl put her hand up

to volunteer – Sharon was surprised because this girl had never prayed in front of a group before. Her hand was trembling even when she put it up. She managed to mumble a one-line prayer that was pretty much incoherent to the rest of the group, and that was it, but the point was she had taken a step. That is quite a strong and public declaration of faith. She had already chosen to come to a part of our programme that was faith-based, and from there she had further singled herself out and said a prayer in front of the others. What a great step of faith!

We see glimpses of this openness to Jesus, and it's little by little. It happens all the time. Another girl, when she first came to e:merge, made it very clear to us that she didn't believe in God. She said that straight out, and we were like, that's fine. No problem. Then after being here just a couple of days, she asked Niki, 'How does somebody become a Christian then? What do you do?' Then she came into Sharon's theology session for the Academy. Not because we'd been preaching at her, but because she'd seen young people who identified themselves as Christians, yet were ordinary people who she actually liked, and who talked about God in a very natural way. People who related to her as a person, not as a potential convert.

So from there, she had evidently been thinking to herself that she should perhaps investigate this a little bit and find out more about it and if it's all not too crazy, then maybe she needs to think about what she should do about it. She came back a couple of days later and told Sharon that she actually prayed the night before to God and said, 'So, if you're real, OK God, I'm going to give you the chance to prove it.' That may be a slightly aggressive prayer style, it may not be the words on the laminated bookmark entitled 'The Sinner's Prayer' that you bought at the Christian bookshop for 49p, but the point is, she's taken a step. She's just opened herself up to the idea that Jesus is real. She's on a journey.

We have to have more than one yardstick here for measuring success, because otherwise we wouldn't last. It would be no good us looking for conventional 'conversions' because we'd then miss the real, messy, unconventional ways that young people are truly and necessarily, starting to engage with God. We have young people all the time who are not committing necessarily, but who are starting to be open and believe maybe that there might be a God, and that some of what we're saying to them makes sense. A few months pass and we'll hear them in conversation with another young person, saying, 'Well, since I decided to be a Christian, I . . .' We think, hang on a minute, when did that happen?

It doesn't matter when it happened. The point is they've made the step and no, I can't date it, and they themselves might not know exactly when it happened because it was gradual, but they have made it. And what's more, it wasn't a snap decision. It wasn't something they were pressured into at a one-off event. They have taken their time and worked it through and now they are identifying with Christ and they're saying it themselves: 'This is what I am. I am a Christian.'

We never say to a young person, 'You've said this, or done that, or prayed the other, so now you're a Christian.' That's wrong in so many ways. It's putting pressure on them, when perhaps they've made a step, but they're not ready to identify themselves as 'Christian'. It's defining them, or boxing them, when they need to have the space to work it out for themselves, so we wait until they tell us, or they use that word about themselves.

Sometimes I think the church has almost made it too easy to label someone as having 'become a Christian' by saying a little prayer in a moment of interest, emotion or conviction, but in a weird way, we make it hard for them to actually come close to God because we put so many stipulations around it once that decision is made.

Niki's diary, 6 October 2005

A group of the girls heard me swear today. Kirsty was there and Claire, too. It was only 'shit' which is nothing, but they were quite surprised – they all suddenly went dead quiet. Then once they'd got over it, they decided it was hilarious, and they gave me absolute hell about it. I was a bit annoyed to be honest, because they don't pull each other up for swearing, so it felt a bit like double standards. I said to them, 'Yeah, when you hear me swear, it isn't nice because you know Niki doesn't swear.'

I'm not sure they really take that in, in the sense of it having any relevance to their own language and behaviour. One of them told Sarah, and she absolutely loved it – I think the idea that polite, respectable Niki has become so integrated into the Bradford 4 culture that she now walks around swearing like a trooper really appeals to her. No one notices when anyone else says that – it kind of doesn't count as swearing – but when I do it, it's suddenly a big deal!

Yan

When Niki arrived, I think she was challenged in herself because she saw some of the young people that we described as our 'strong Christians' acting in ways that were completely different from, say, youth groups she had worked with in more affluent areas. We saw her grappling with it. She would ask, 'How can that person be a Christian when they drink, or fight, or argue, or swear?' And we would have to ask, 'Is not doing those things what makes you a Christian? Or is it the fact that you have dedicated your life to Jesus, and you are trying to understand and follow and relate to him, even when it keeps going wrong?'

Again, it's obvious when you set it down on paper, but it's something our mindsets get into the habit of – judging whether people are Christian or not by what they do. Over a number of months, we could actually see how Niki's mind was starting to work and how she started to engage with this culture, with this expression of Christianity.

Bringing Christ into this environment is challenging, it's tough to start with, and then to say to young people, don't smoke, don't drink, don't have sex before marriage – you know, it's a complete shock, and compared to some of the things going on in their lives that they are battling with, that can be relatively irrelevant. If three generations of your family are alcoholic, believe me, you don't want to drink. You don't want to become like that. But everything is a battle. So somebody coming along and saying, 'Now you've prayed once to God, you have to stop drinking,' is coming from completely the wrong direction. It's still rooted in the expectation that we understand these young people's lives. And we don't. Not until we've spent time with them and seen it for ourselves.

A fair few of our young people who are Christian –
who have prayed and made a decision for themselves,
and talked about it – they do still swear, they do smoke,
they do have sex before marriage, sometimes for quite
a while after they have embraced faith. They do all
these things that Christianity says you cannot do. And
yet they are followers of Christ. They have very real
experiences with the Lord and they want to move on
in faith.

I'm not in any way saying that personal holiness
is not important. It is vital, and it is definitely one of
the ways in which we can bless God, draw closer to
him and become more like Christ, as well as modelling
positive, healthy behaviours. But the thing is, my
personal holiness is between me and God and whoever
I ask to be close to me and make myself accountable to.
It's not up to you or anyone who doesn't know me to
tell me what I should and shouldn't be doing in life.

Aside from everything else, it is only God who can
make us holy anyway – we are justified by grace,
not by acts – and holiness is something we can
aspire to, precisely because God has set us free from
condemnation. The possibility of being holy at all is his
gift to us. In the Bible, objects and places were holy
because God was there – not because of what anyone
had done or not done. Mount Sinai, for example,
became holy because God was there (see Exodus 19).
True holiness is fighting for justice, loving the poor
and providing for people's needs, because that is what
constitutes the kingdom of God – that is what God is
like, that is his style, his community. So our priority
will always be walking with God and working for the
benefit of people who are marginalised.

Our job is to outline God's way, God's character,
to these young people, and to encourage them, not

condemn them, not lay expectations on them that they can't yet meet – because that's a sure way to turn them away from God. We will get round to showing them lots of the ways to live that God has set out. But firstly, we want to tell them about God's love. We want them to know that he accepts them just as they are. Even if they never change, he has already died for them, already done everything, already fallen in love with them. Everything starts with the unconditional love of God.

Niki's diary, 14 October 2005

Julie still has this horrible stuff happening to her at home. Her uncle bought some really nice presents for her and her mum at the weekend, but then he stayed at the pub till late. When he got home he was really drunk, and after her mum had gone to bed, he beat Julie up and told her she was useless and said it was her fault that her mum was in such a state and called her really disgusting names. She gets frustrated, really frustrated and upset, because she can't even explain what is happening and why and how it makes her feel. She doesn't have the words for it. She just says, 'I don't know, I don't know,' over and over. We went for another walk last Thursday, and it was amazing – she just talked and talked for about an hour. We got so much further than all the formal one to ones that I've had with her in the office. At one stage I asked, 'Is this sort of helping?' and she said, 'I don't know,' but later she texted me, 'it was nice talking to you, you helped me understand things better'.

Sharon told them that we sometimes think God expects us to get down on our knees and plead for forgiveness and he's kind of standing there thinking, 'Yeah, keep it up just a bit longer, then I might forgive you.' It's not like that. She said, if anything, it's the opposite. God is eager and he's waiting for any kind of sign that we are sorry – anything that shows him we realise we were wrong. He's not waiting for the big, dramatic begging. When you can be bothered to say, 'Soz God,' he'll take that, because the relationship between you and him is what's important to him and whenever it's not there, he is longing to have it back. God doesn't need a lot of convincing. He *likes* forgiving you. It's what he's all about.

There is absolutely no frame of reference for teaching the young people about the reality of God. It's not just a question of shifting their preconceptions, it's creating a whole new concept. It's like trying to teach someone to swim when they've never seen water before. They don't know what 'wet' means, or how water moves or feels, or how you can get in it and get out of it. It requires a paradigm shift. A lot of our job is starting to create an environment where the young people can simply start to believe that God is on their side, because nobody else has ever been on their side so why would he be?

Niki's diary, 21 October 2005

We have started doing this suggestion box thing at drop in. We have a question of the week, and the young people can write their responses on a piece of paper and put them in the box. Then we open it at the end of the week, and see what has been put in. It's a bit of fun really, but it gives a really interesting insight into what people are thinking. Our question this week was, if you could ask God a question what would it be? I've copied down some of the responses:

- Why do you make things so hard?
- Why do so few people work in areas like this?
- How long am I going to live?
- What will heaven be like?
- Why do you not speak more clearly?
- To have a better brother
- When will I die?
- Where did you come from?
- Why is life a riddle?
- What could we do about AIDS? Is there something specific?
- Why is life so hard?
- When is Jesus coming back?
- Why?
- Why is there so much poverty?
- When will money grow on trees?
- When will I get to meet you?
- Which hurt more, the spear in your side or the three hours without your father?

Yan

We had a young man on the Academy whose family had come over from the Caribbean. He is a great success story for us because he completed the Academy and is now studying for an NVQ at a local sixth form college. We were there for him educationally because we helped him through the Academy, but all the time he was there, there were major stresses happening in his family life.

His mother had cancer and his father was in prison. At one stage, there was the possibility that his family would be deported. He does not describe himself as a Christian, but we believe he experienced a piece of God's salvation and kingdom in the fact that through e:merge he was able to develop his qualifications and job skills, and also that he received support through that horrendously difficult time.

Another lad we worked with was from a healthy background and stable family, but not a massive achiever in terms of academic qualifications. He came on the Academy at the age of twenty and now works as an outdoor pursuits instructor up in Scotland. He had never lived away from home and would never have had the confidence or opportunity to get into that kind of employment without the equipping he received from e:merge. He absolutely loves his job, and that is part of God's gift to him in his life.

It's only in the last 100 years or so that the church's perceptions of salvation have centred around the spiritual sense of being saved, and saying the prayer of salvation. Historically, the church was about salvation in the broadest – and truest – sense, which was hospitality. Creating, living and welcoming people into the kingdom of God, which is a place of care, provision and healing. The church provided hospitals, houses, schools, had a central place in society for meeting people's needs. It didn't separate people's spiritual needs from their emotional, practical or economic needs. It was all one. I think there's a call from God out to the church that says salvation is to care for people. This is the church's heritage. It's a rich heritage and it needs recapturing.

Jesus definitely told us to preach the good news, and to make disciples, but he also made it very clear that part of our heavenly role on earth is to provide care of all kinds to people who are vulnerable and needy.

Niki's diary, 22 October 2005

I prayed with my girls in cell group at Xstream last night. It was the first time I've ever done it. I got them all on their knees – ten of them – knee to knee, very, very close and I made them hold little fingers. At first they were like, 'This is embarrassing, Niki. No one else is doing this.' I just said, 'Now I want you to bow your heads down.'

Sometimes I lack self esteem and I lack confidence and I think, I can't do this. I've had a bad day, bad week, personal stuff might be going wrong and it does, it affects my job. But yesterday, the topic was faith and they all said, 'I need more faith for God to help me in my life.' None of them said with what, but I know for a lot of them, they are quite horrendous things. I think really, deep inside of me, there was a huge concern for these girls and I wasn't thinking about whether I had the confidence or not, I just thought, they said they want more faith and they want God to help and so I have to pray. So I just prayed that God would help them and they were still while I prayed. They didn't pray out loud with me, but they all had their eyes shut and they were very still.

Note

1   Skills for Life Survey, DfES 2003/Annual Population Survey, NOMIS, as reported by the Economic Policy Team in the Department of Regeneration, Bradford.

11

The Three Rs – Rules, Rebellion and aRriving On Time

Niki's diary, 24 October 2005

Our hearts were in our mouths today, because Monday is the day Darren goes to work as a PE instructor at a local school – or doesn't . . . He's on the Academy this year, and he's great, really committed. He's a gifted coach, and he got a one day a week placement helping out with PE at this school not far away. It's the first time he's had any kind of job. His first day was two Mondays ago – or supposed to be – but the school rang up at half ten, going, 'Where's Darren?' John said, 'Isn't he with you? He's not with us,' and they were like, 'No, he hasn't turned up.' John was absolutely gutted.

John put his coat on and went round to see Darren. Darren was sitting at home, head in hands, and when John asked him about it, all he could say was, 'I bottled it. I couldn't do it.'

John got him to ring the school and apologise, and promise to be there the following week. Darren wouldn't have done that off his own back – he had presumed he'd blown it already, but the school gave him another chance.

The following Monday, John decided to go with Darren to the school. The way John explained it, taking an hour to make sure Darren was out of bed and got to his job safely, could be a fulcrum for the rest of Darren's life. If he could just get to the placement the first time, break the fear, then he would keep going, and if he could successfully keep going, then he might get a job there once the placement ended, and if he got a job, then really, the world was opening up for him.

So last week, John went with him, banged on his door, made sure he was up, and Darren got to the school, and stayed for the day, and came back absolutely glowing. Still nervous, but on a real rush that he had managed it. This week, John said to Darren, 'I think you should get there on your own,' and Darren agreed. We all knew it was still a risk, so in staff meeting, we were waiting for John to come in, because he was going to telephone the school to check whether Darren was there. John arrived and was just beaming. He simply said, 'Darren's at his placement,' and we all went, 'Brilliant! Nice one, mate!' with a mixture of excitement and relief.

It's funny. It was the sort of reaction I would have had last year if one of the kids I was working with won a prize or was accepted into Oxbridge or secured a high flying graduate job. This was just turning up for work for a one day a week, unpaid placement. But for Darren, it was just as significant a victory, if not more so.

Yan

For young people who want to engage more strongly with us and with training, we have something called the Academy, which is a structured, year-long programme of training and personal development for a small number of young people – usually between six and ten.

The Academy takes them for that whole year and works with them on personal development, basic skills, communication skills, and also on leadership through the acquisition of a qualification in sports coaching. The Academy is small in terms of numbers but in each of the students' lives it's absolutely enormous. It's key in helping them into life, into employment, into faith, just into some kind of routine and solidity. Because it travels with them for a whole year at quite a crucial point in their life, it has the potential to make a massive difference.

The students come four days a week, Tuesday to Friday, to the classroom we have in the building. We encourage and support them in using the Monday each week to get a work placement – usually related to their sports coaching. Tuesday to Friday, they learn a whole range of skills to do with personal development and getting ready for employment. That might include drugs education, communication skills, self-esteem and assertiveness, work ethic and basic skills. These are all taught by different staff at e:merge. A number of us have teaching qualifications or other relevant professional skills. We will also occasionally have external teachers and facilitators coming in – for example, we had an NHS professional come and talk about diet and healthy living. They got the students to keep food diaries and showed them how to make healthy things like porridge

and smoothies. It was quite a revelation for some of
the young people who literally ate fish and chips every
day.

We also teach about ethics, and there are theology
sessions where we teach about God's character. Then
in the afternoons they have coaching drills and more
on the sports side. Some of that is led by previous
graduates of the Academy who we have trained up
as facilitators. It's up to each individual student which
sports they choose to train for. Although, as one would
expect, football is always popular, we have also had
students electing for netball, rugby, cricket and gym/
personal training.

I think the Academy is an unusual programme because
of the way it works with young people individually
and spends time on personal development as well
as skills. That's very different from some approaches
where the objective is to get a large number of young
people through your module or training course as
quickly as you can. We were doing individual learning
plans well before it was recognised that was the way to
tailor learning to the students. I suppose it's all part of
our wider ethos of saying, we will spend as long as it
takes to make real differences in young people's lives.
We offer a combination of the specific and the holistic.
They will hopefully all get at least a level one coaching
qualification at the end – but they will also, much more
importantly, have the self-awareness, communication
skills and understanding of the working world to be
more successful in dealing with life, especially in getting
employment.

We do a lot of work on communication, and we do
a lot of work on self-esteem. You don't realise it unless
you've been without it, or known someone without

it, but self-esteem is the basis of everything. It's not a luxury. It's where all understanding of behaviour, both your own and other people's, stems from.

We had a student on the Academy who had an argument with a friend who had then called him a lot of names. This was an older, very influential friend, and the student was devastated to feel that he had lost that friendship. His confidence plummeted, and he became quite uncooperative that morning, disrupting the lesson. John was teaching and asked, 'What is going on with you this morning?' and got him to talk about the incident. When the student had explained, John said, 'Right, let's have a look at this, and let's have a look at your self-esteem. How are you feeling?'

'Crap,' said the student.

'Why? Because you've believed those things that person said to you. When you think about the statements they made, are they true? No they're not. You know that, and actually they know that as well. So let's think about why that person said those things to you.'

They talked about it as a group, and discovered that it had occurred just when our student had completed a short course for which he got a coaching certificate. So it didn't take a rocket scientist to work out that the other person's reaction might partly be influenced by jealousy. They discussed how perhaps that person was feeling threatened because the student had achieved a certificate they didn't have – they were feeling overtaken by someone younger than them. From that discussion about self-esteem, through to understanding behaviours, we got to the bottom of the problem, and from there, the student was able to feel better about himself and focus on learning again.

If you have serious problems with your own self-esteem, it's almost impossible to have a balanced view of other people's behaviours, or to motivate yourself. If you want to look at it economically, we're building self-esteem because that will be a significant factor in getting young people into employment, which in turn will contribute to the economy of this community. Looking at it otherwise, you can say that we're teaching people to believe in themselves, because every person has the same value and deserves to know that.

Sometimes, the economic reasoning is something that we take particular care to explain to the parents of the potential Academy students. They will often say, why should my son or daughter take a £50 a week training allowance from the Academy when he or she could be working at a supermarket for £180 a week? We discovered early on that it is really worth making contact with parents where we can. We explain that this year of lower earnings will establish skills and behaviours that will enable the young person to earn more in the future, and to have broader employment prospects than if they went straight into working in a paid but low-skilled job. This has had an impact in that we now have parents approaching us to find out whether the Academy is the right kind of intervention for their teenage son or daughter.

The other unusual aspect of the Academy of course is that it caters for the very people who cannot, at that point in their lives, cope with a more intense learning intervention. We generally have students who have dropped out of school, or left without any qualifications, and they will not really be able to cope with the demands of further education colleges yet, because they don't have the discipline or confidence. The Academy comes between those things and offers something that is a tailor-made challenge which they are more likely to achieve, and which is going to give them useful, practical skills in a context and environment comfortable enough for them to be able to learn in.

Students have usually come to drop-ins or engaged with other e:merge activities previous to applying for the Academy, so they know us and they know the place. Often they know someone else who has previously been in the Academy. So the learning all takes place in a very safe environment for the students. We do everything in an environment that doesn't resemble school – it's a room set out informally, and in a building they know is a youth project rather than an educational establishment. That all helps young people who have never learned successfully before to start learning.

Often we will have students who say to us, 'I wish school had been like this – I would have learnt something then!' because they are experiencing a completely different atmosphere. They feel respected here, and they are in an environment where they are expected to succeed rather than fail. Throughout e:merge, whether it's playing football in the park during a detached session, or conducting a lesson at the Academy, we create an environment where everyone is positive. No one has a go or criticises. Sometimes it's hard work to maintain that attitude, but we know it's vitally important. It's all about what you can get right rather than what has gone wrong. For a lot of our students, school was simply a place where you constantly received the message that you were stupid. In some cases, that message has come from teachers, other pupils, or simply from the fact that you knew you weren't able to keep up with the work.

At the Academy, they are being taught in small groups, in a conversational style which enables them to have a lot of input. That's how we are set up. This particularly helps students who have learning disabilities or behavioural difficulties. We are well aware that some of the young people we now work with have assaulted teachers – and we completely support the fact that teachers should not have to put up with that. We also support the fact that those young people still need to learn, and we are prepared to help them.

We know that some people will say we are being soft on these young people – there will always be that criticism. Some will say that setting ourselves up to be as little like school as possible is essentially supporting the fact that young people have rebelled against school. It isn't. I wish that every one of the young people I work with had stayed at school and completed their GCSEs. I would have liked them to have respected their teachers, have had the self-discipline to do all their work, and have never treated their fellow pupils badly. That's not the reality. We are dealing with young people who have not succeeded in the mainstream system. You can't put that right by putting them into another similar system where they will also fail. We teach students respect and self-discipline and positive attitudes to others and themselves. We can only do that successfully if they are in a place where they listen to us. So we create that place first, meet the students where they're at, and then start building things back up again.

We regularly gather evaluation material on the Academy, and we recently carried out an exercise to contact previous Academy graduates 6 months after they had left. In one cohort, 90 per cent said they now viewed education positively, and also that they would consider returning to formal education. One hundred per cent of students who completed the Academy said they wished they had done better at school.

Niki's diary, 27 October 2005

The Academy students all had to do a presentation to each other today. It was a presentation of three minutes where they had to stand up and say their name, age, where they lived, and who their favourite person was – famous or otherwise. They had to produce three PowerPoint slides to show while they were talking. Most of them did it fine – a few nerves, but managed it. But when it got to Peter's turn – he's a big, seventeen year old lad – he was absolutely terrified and he refused to do the presentation unless he was allowed to do it with a coat on his head. John was like, 'Mate, you don't need to do that,' but Peter insisted – he literally could not do it if he could see the other people in the room. So he got his coat and put it on, with his hood pulled right across his face, so he could only just see the slides he was showing, and he did the presentation with his voice muffled up inside. Hilarious! The thing is, at school, he wouldn't have been allowed to do that, and he would have been chucked out of the classroom or something. But here, you make the challenge as small as you can, until it's possible for the young person to achieve it, and then you celebrate it when they do, and only after that do you move on to another small, achievable challenge.

There's another lad who's really keen to do the Academy next year. Steven. He's the one who caused havoc in North Yorkshire at John's sports camp. He has seen people do the Academy and wants a go himself. However, Yan and John have discussed it with him and said that they just don't think he's ready to make a success of it yet. He doesn't have enough control over his own behaviours still, or even the possibility for that. He hangs out at e:merge a lot of the time which is great, and one day he'll hopefully be ready for something like the Academy, but for now he's too much of a handful. The other day he was really winding everyone up and being hyper and destructive. I heard Yan eventually say to him, 'Steven, I love you. But I've had enough now.'

Yan

We interview the young people who apply to the Academy quite rigorously. We know it's not for everyone, and we don't want to set them up to fail. It's worse for a young person to start the course and then not be able to finish it, than not start at all. If they don't start, they are in the same position they were. If they start and don't finish, then that will be a failure for them, a backwards step. We also do tests to measure their literacy and numeracy skills, so that we know exactly what kind of support they need, in which areas. We try and do everything we can to make it likely that the student will succeed, but at the same time, we're not a pushover.

Someone once said to John, 'Isn't your kind of youth work just countenancing young people's rebellion?' Unfortunately, that's a common misconception. There's a feeling that youth workers are so completely on the young person's side that they only see things from their point of view and don't challenge behaviour or assumptions any more. That's rubbish. We don't make a big thing of rules and regulations, because we are primarily about the relationship, but anyone who is working constructively with young people will have a structure of rules and boundaries.

The more deeply the young people get involved with us, the more they know they are expected to behave to certain standards – everything is proportionate. When we go out on detached work, of course, we are on their turf so we can't expect them to behave in any particular way. We only address something if it's disrespectful to us, or if it's illegal. It's similar for the drop-in sessions, except that we ensure a few requirements are met because the young people are coming through our doors and are getting some benefit – appropriate use of the computers is an obvious one, and young people will be banned from attending if they view pornography or use other inappropriate sites. Even with this, the important thing is to explain why we have rules, rather than suggesting we are trying to force them to meet some kind of standard that we have set arbitrarily.

Yes, if you come to Xstream on a Friday night, you might see some young lad wandering in and out, or texting in the middle of a talk. Big deal. We would rather have him there and texting than not there at all. But if he is abusive to a staff member, or another young person, he will be asked to leave and potentially banned for a period of time.

One of the absolutely vital areas for the Academy is helping young people make themselves ready for the world of work. There are things we need to work on with them that would be unnecessary for some people of their age. Many will be averse to being told what to do by anyone, including a boss at a place of work, because that to them is equal to being disrespected. They have not learnt about working together and organisational relationships. So we have to reinforce the realities of the working environment in the way we organise the

Academy. One thing we have introduced is a system of fines. We set out at the beginning of each year what is unacceptable, and we agree with all the students what those things are and what the levels of sanction should be. If they break the rules, we fine them – £1 or £2 – because money talks. They get a small training allowance for being on the Academy, so we deduct the fine from that if they cannot pay it on the spot. After a certain number of fines, they will get a verbal warning, then a written warning, and they all know that the ultimate sanction is not being able to continue with the Academy.

There are a few people who we have had to release from the Academy. Once you have gone through all the steps of fining the student, of sitting down and talking through with them their behaviour and their circumstances, and you've given them verbal and then written warnings, and they are still not achieving the minimum standard you need from them, well, you have to face facts. If they are consistently breaking the rules, you have to enforce the ultimate sanction, which is cancelling their participation. Again, you have to ensure that the whole way you do it is not about a power play or getting rid of them – it's all about ensuring that the group as a whole is able to have an experience of getting through the course. It's only happened three times in the four years we've been running the Academy – and each time, the student concerned has been absolutely gutted. There have been tears, and more promises that it won't happen again, but you have to enforce it. And each time as well, there has been recognition from the rest of the group that that person must be released, because otherwise it wouldn't be fair and it would be detrimental to the remainder of the students and their chances of success.

The thing that they will often find different in our system of rules, compared to say school or home, is that they are not rooted in how we – educated, older people – think young people should behave. They are rooted in the reality of what the Academy is all about which is training young people in the skills and attitudes that will help them get employment.

So when we say, no swearing, it's not because we personally think that swearing is wrong. It's because they will not hold down a job if they cannot control their language or understand how certain words and phrases are received by other people. We are very strict about punctuality. Why? Not because we personally think it's a cardinal sin to be late, but because the reality of the working world says, if you can't turn up reliably, regularly and on time, you will not last in employment. We explain all this to the students from the start, and they know where we're coming from.

The students also know that our rules always flow from relationship. We don't make our relationship with them contingent on obeying the rules. No way. We still relate even to people we have thrown out of drop-ins, or banned from the building. That is separate from addressing their behaviour. The rules are there because we care what happens to the young people.

It's vitally important, once you've set up a policy, to stick to it. You can't say, 'We'll fine you if you do x,' and then they do x and we give them another chance. In the same way that these kids have had broken promises all their lives, they've also had empty threats. Though it might feel negative at the time, you have to enforce it, because then you are doing what you said you would do. At last they have a sense of continuity, of consistency instead of chaos.

Young people like boundaries. People will say that's cheesy, but it's true. A young person craves order, comfort and security. They want the main aspects of their life to be stable and secure. They need to know what people expect from them, and how they will be treated. It's only from that basis that they can feel secure enough to experiment and reach out and do new things. With young people like those we relate to, whose lives are often full of insecurity – in terms of family, education, personal safety, relationships – they need a lot of stability from somewhere to help build everything back up again.

We want to have structures in place that teach them how to treat others well. Not just that, but also to stick up for themselves if someone else is treating them badly. It works both ways. If you've had no rules enforced in your life, then not only do you not know how to treat others, but also, you have no frame of reference for how other people should treat you. We work on assertiveness because some of them are so used to being treated badly they don't realise there is a choice. There's nothing between being badly treated and becoming aggressive yourself.

People can talk a lot about young people's rebellion, but the fact is, here, too many young people conform. They conform to the expectations they have grown up with – that they won't really amount to anything, that they won't get a decent job, that they can't control their behaviours or be responsible in how they treat each other. Actually, we want them to rebel against that – to decide that they can be different, they can make a success out of their lives, they can be positive role models for their peers. Giving them the right rules, with meaningful consequences consistently enforced, is one way that we can contribute.

Niki's diary, 5 November 2005

Dave got prayed for at Xstream last night and he came up to me afterwards, looking completely ecstatic. He went, 'I felt the Holy Spirit, Niki! It was better than drugs!' It was brill, and it made me laugh. If anything does feel better than drugs, well, Dave should know.

12

Measuring Jelly

Niki's diary, 7 November 2005

Claire bought a handbag at the weekend – she showed it to me today. It sounds like a minor thing, but it's really significant. A lot of girls don't have handbags around here – they have pockets in their tracksuit trousers and maybe sports bags or something, but nothing as feminine as a handbag. She's just started clipping her fringe up out of her eyes as well. She still kind of hides behind massive baggy jumpers and trousers, but still, I think it shows she is becoming more confident and taking an interest in her appearance.

Some of the girls have noticed, too, I think and they are being quite encouraging, suggesting going shopping with her to buy some more shapely tops. I was really chuffed. It's such a great thing to see them operating together as friends and encouragers. It's hopefully a foundation for a long future of positive relationships.

I'm starting to learn how to notice the tiny things that point to progress being made in some of these kids' lives. You can't only take encouragement from the big things like I would have done before – kids becoming Christians, getting brilliant jobs, going to university. The big positive things are few and far between. So you learn to read the little things. When you know what complete crap these girls have gone through, you can get very excited about things that people outside might think are really insignificant, like buying a handbag. Thank you, God.

Yan

One of the things that has really grown in the youth work sector – and perhaps the voluntary sector generally – over the last few years is the sense that even very soft outcomes can start to be measured or quantified in some way. By 'soft outcomes' I mean things like: how many of the young people are showing signs of increased self-confidence; how many are using drugs less, or drinking less than they used to; how many are making a contribution, or speaking up for the first time; how many of them have stopped hanging out with people who were a negative influence. Sometimes trying to quantify these things is a bit like trying to measure jelly.

We want to be run on sound business principles, and part of that is that it's important to know what our successes are, and to measure them in some way. For most of us, counting doesn't come easy. We are very person-focused, so we are not primarily interested in whether more than 60 per cent of our students eventually go on to either employment or full-time training. What we're much more interested in is whether Abbi gets past her debilitating shyness, whether Paul learns to turn up on time, whether Shelly has the guts to apply for that job which we all know she could be good at. Those are some of the most important effects our work can have. So we have to find ways of measuring and pointing out these changes and successes to our partners and our funders, as well as noticing them ourselves.

The funding organisations we rely on for much of our income quite rightly expect us to demonstrate that we are using their money wisely and effectively, especially when it is public money. However, the difficulty with funding bodies is – rightly in many ways – the importance of demonstrating value for money and the concrete benefits which the funding will have or has had. The main problem is not that we don't achieve the benefits they are looking for, but that it takes a long time. There is a whole period that is spent getting the trust of the young people – especially for those who are marginalised and excluded from mainstream provision – and you simply cannot achieve the more measurable benefits until that trust has been established. There needs to be a way of securing funding for that kind of pre-measurable period where the foundations are being laid, because without them you will not build a house – or if you do, the house will soon fall down, and your money will have been wasted.

We have for a long time carried out evaluations of the Academy by contacting Graduates at 6 months and 12 months after graduation to see what they are now doing in their lives, and crucially, whether they are in some kind of education or employment. We have also started using a tool called the 'Richter Scale' which is a format that helps us measure softer outcomes.

It is important that youth workers and project workers learn how to monitor and evaluate successes. When Diarmuid or I write a grant application, we won't claim that if someone gives us some funding then miracles will happen overnight, but we will show that e:merge teaches young people life skills and gives them some confidence, which in turn makes it more likely that they will get some education and eventually be able to sustain employment, and therefore start contributing to the economy. It's tackling individual poverty – micro-poverty if you like – and if we keep doing that, we will eventually be affecting the whole area. It takes time, and it's small, but it's definitely there.

Niki's diary, 8 November 2005

A friend of one of the volunteers came to see the project and was surprised that we didn't talk more about Jesus to the kids. I just think you can't separate it out. It's not just the talk. Young people don't normally come to know Jesus because we've told them about Jesus. It's more because we've demonstrated in our lives what Jesus is like. So, for example, we've demonstrated that we're interested in the young people's lives – that our desire is for their wholeness, not just to turn them into Christians or people like us.

People just don't understand about the lives of the young people here – what do they want me to say to someone I meet on detached – 'Yes, I know you have a drug problem, and your girlfriend has just got pregnant and doesn't know whether to have an abortion, because neither of you has anywhere safe to live, but the point is, I need to tell you about Jesus . . .'?

I suppose I've really only started to see it myself, but there is spiritual growth here, it's just that it doesn't always look how a conventional church would expect it to look.

Yan

You look at this city and you can see that it has been neglected. It has been dumped on many times over the years. There is good stuff happening now – they are ripping a load of really nasty buildings out of the town centre, which is great, rebuilding and making it more of a place with a heart. And there are good churches around and some good Christian influences, people praying and working for the good of this city. But when you think back over the years of industrial revolution – of exploitation of the workers, of immigrants sweeping in and hardly being looked after, of generations of poverty and lack of opportunity – that is what you are grappling with spiritually.

Over the years that I've worked here, I've come to realise that salvation in every sense takes place over generations rather than being a one-off event. Our spiritual battle is against the forces that have ground Bradford and BD4 down over a long period, and salvation will come on a long-term schedule, after a lot of gritty, dedicated fighting. Take employment and productivity, for example. Bradford's gross domestic product (GDP) is one of the lowest in the UK. GDP is driven by productivity and employment, and again, in both these categories, Bradford is near the bottom of the table. Employment depends on people being available to work and able to work – having the skills and experience, and also the ability to hold down a job. We know employers locally who say they will not employ young people from Bradford 4 because they don't trust them to stick at the job. They have had experience of this, which has meant a waste of time, energy and money in recruiting people who then do not stay, or are fired.

If we can teach young people to read better, to have the work-readiness skills and work ethic to hold down a job, we are starting in that way to turn the tide, even if it takes them some time to find that job. If we can express the love of God to young people, and they can start to trust in other people and in God again, they might never come to say the prayer or come to express faith in the way that we expect them to, but they will see a glimpse of the goodness of God. We are now starting to work with the children of some of the young people we worked with when we first arrived, and that's really interesting. Those children are definitely more open, whether or not their parents had 'successes' with us. Because God has prepared the ground in their parents' lives, we now have a better opportunity to work with their children and we have more opportunity to share the gospel and to communicate the love of Christ.

It is our mission to work with God to help improve every aspect of the lives of the young people here in Bradford 4. Mission is about commitment, and it is generational. Short-term mission is easier, of course it is. We have to have vision that sustains us over years, and we pray constantly for the spiritual insight to know that God is changing things here, whether or not we see regular outward signs.

Niki's diary, 12 November 2005

I had this feeling I should text Julie yesterday evening, saying to read Psalm 91. It's all about God being your strength and your protection, and I texted it and said, 'that's for you'. Then today she came over to my house and told me that the beating had happened again, just before I sent her that text. She just asked, 'When, Niki? When is God going to protect me?'

The first thing it said in the advert for this job was, 'Have you got faith for the faithless?' I thought I did have when I applied. I'm not sure I do now.

13

It's a Girl Thing

Yan

When new staff arrive here, you can't really tell them exactly what their job will be. Obviously, you give them a job description to start with, but where they end up depends on what happens – where their gifts start to show, and what God puts on their heart. It's important to let people discover that kind of thing and support them when they start having ideas and visions for any part of the project, because then they are owning the project more and more – they are becoming an integral part of it and doing the things that God has enabled them to do. It also means they are becoming more committed to the work and to the young people.

For John, it was very obvious that he had a gift for sport and a way of communicating through that. So he started up the Academy and leads that for us. For Niki, after a few months of her being here, we saw her starting to develop a heart for the girls work, which was fantastic because she was someone who was young and girlie and unmarried, who the young women could relate to.

For me, the girls are harder to work with. They can be very controlling and rough – and they often drink and swear and shout more than the boys do. But when you see the way they are used to being treated, it's not surprising. I was in the minibus once taking a few lads to a project on the other side of Bradford. As we were driving, there were two or three young girls walking by the road – girls who were known to the guys in my minibus. As soon as they saw the girls, the lads opened the windows and started yelling abuse – calling out to them to lift up their tops so they could see their breasts, preceding almost every word in the sentence with a swear word or an abusive term for a woman. The girls weren't surprised by it, and in fact they gave back as good as they got, but in a way that made it worse because it showed they were used to being treated in that way and found it normal.

It's vitally important for us to treat the young women with respect. So many of the girls we work with have been through absolute nightmares. I really care about them, but it would be inappropriate for any man in our project to work closely with the girls, so if ever there is a one-to-one situation or a need for someone to have specific input, I will refer the young woman to Sharon or Niki.

Niki's diary, 19 November 2005

I'm beginning to see a lot more of the main group of girls I know outside work time. I have them round for a cup of tea or a chat sometimes, or we go for a walk or to a café and I buy them a coffee. Sometimes if I'm going shopping, I ask one of them if they want to come with me. I'm always careful to be appropriate and professional about it of course. Most of the girls I hang out with outside e:merge are eighteen or more, and I know most of their mums as well. If they are younger, I always have two of them with me and speak to their parents to say where we are going beforehand. I think that's important because although I'm not going to do anything irresponsible, it shows I respect them enough to be sure to follow all our policies and guidelines properly. They need a bit of respect.

Yan is so brilliant with the young lads – very fun and fatherly – but he's very aware that with the girls he can't have the same kind of informal friendship, for professional reasons. If they need any kind of individual attention, he will always refer them to Sharon or me. In some ways, the girls are more complicated I suppose, and he doesn't always understand them. They are not as open and up front as the boys.

The young girls I've spent time with come across as very confident, even strong and bolshie, but they're not at all. It's a cover up. It's only now I'm really getting to know them that I realise that. Some people think they're sex obsessed, which is unfair and really a stereotype. I don't think the teenagers round here necessarily have more sex or more sexual partners than teenagers from more well to do backgrounds, it's just that it's more obvious – they don't have the sense of imposed social niceties to hide it.

In fact, statistics show the teenage conception rate to be roughly the same in more well to do areas than more deprived places like Bradford, but the difference is that the abortion rate in the well to do areas, particularly the South East, is much higher.[1] The general conclusion is that young women in more affluent or socially mobile areas have other aspirations, and make choices between pregnancy and other opportunities. Somewhere like here, young women see pregnancy as their only choice.

A lot of the girls will have babies early on in life. They won't necessarily wait until they are in a committed relationship, certainly not a permanent one. And they won't necessarily think about it a lot. To them, having a baby is a way to feel significant, to take some kind of control in your life, and to create something that is your own – a baby, who will love you. That's very important. It's like a rite of passage, signifying that they are not children any more. It's also a way to get away from your household, because you're more likely to get housing with a child than as a single person. So for some of the girls with really horrendous home situations, it's a very effective escape route. It can also be a way of avoiding the decision of what to do with their lives – shall I get a job? Shall I study? Oh, I'll have a baby. And that kind of makes the decision for them.

When you say 'teenage pregnancy', many people will automatically think it's a really bad thing. They don't bother to think more broadly about the situation these girls are in. What if, actually, becoming a mother is the thing that makes a young woman think about her responsibilities, the way she acts, and that ends up being a positive force in her life – because for some girls, that can happen. Not that I would recommend early pregnancy or single parenthood as a sensible life choice for teenage girls, but actually I think we should also face the facts that it's real, it happens, and it's pointless to demonise those young women or suggest that they are all the same, all having the same experience. If we really want to help reduce the amount of teenage pregnancies, we need to create a community where there are alternative paths in life that they can realistically take.

For many of these girls, it is hard to find role models of women who have taken control of their lives in a positive way, or who have broken away from the fairly narrow expectations of the communities here. Many of their mothers will have had children very early, and outside of stable relationships. Many women they see around or know will have drug dependencies, or will be in abusive relationships. There are very few who are financially independent, or who have good jobs, or have demonstrated a desire to educate themselves. Not that those are the only ways for a woman to value herself – being a mother is the most precious gift and responsibility in the world. But the point is, it's the choice, the sense of 'I can decide my own life' which is really missing. So you have to start by creating even just the idea that these girls can , if they want to, be something different from most of the women around them, that there is the possibility to break out of the cycle.

I also think that they haven't got the power or the confidence to make wise choices. In fact, I think the girls often don't realise that having sex or not can be a choice for them, that early pregnancy is a choice, not a given. When they do something, it's not because they've thought it through and that's what they've decided. It's much more that they just do what is expected, what everyone else does, and that's life, isn't it?

One of the young women here, Abbi, has been coming to drop ins and Xstream for about a year now. She told me she's made a decision that she's not going to have sex again. I don't know whether that's until she's married or what, but it's enough just to say, for the moment, that's what she has decided. She can see that she has made some silly choices in the past. She's been pushed into it and not enjoyed sex because the guy's put pressure on her and that's the only reason it's happened. Now she's got more confidence to actually say that she respects herself more than that. That she isn't going to let someone do that to her any more. It's brave of her, because the guys can be quite nasty if you refuse sex, and say you're frigid, or the rumours can go round about you.

When we talk about sex and try to educate the girls here — well, the lads, too — we start from a different place from where I might have started elsewhere. It's about being standard bearers for what is right, but also having bags and bags of grace when things go wrong. From my point of view, I talk to them about not having sex outside marriage, because I really believe that's the best and healthiest thing for them. Like if we do a session on smoking, I'll tell them it's not good for them and give the reasons why. Same with sex. I know the reality — that many of them will not do what I'm recommending, certainly not 100 per cent of it, or not at the moment, but that's not a reason to stop saying it. Alongside that, we talk about infections and pregnancy and safe sex

– so we're being realistic about where the young people are at as well as giving them something to potentially aim for. It's not all or nothing.

Anyway, you can't just tell the young people what to do. Even the ones with a Christian faith. You can't just say, 'it says so in the Bible'. That doesn't wash. They are so far away from the concept of somebody else knowing what's best for them – or doing something because it's written in a book they don't really understand or know who wrote – and anyway, I think it's good that they ask why, and what the reasons are behind things. A lot of Christians from my kind of background have just been told what to do and not to do, without the reasons why, especially living a sex free life. Then, when their lifestyle is challenged, their faith is very thin – they easily fall away because there's no rationale, just a rule.

When you deal with moral issues properly, explaining why you believe what you believe, then even kids that have grown up without any sense of boundaries or moral codes can start to see that's a good way to be. So I will say to them, 'The reason I think it's a good thing to wait until you're married to have sex is because it gives you some self esteem and confidence to respect yourself, respect your body, respect someone else's body. It avoids health risks and unwanted pregnancies. Sex is a brilliant and precious thing, so it's for someone you trust and you know will treat you well. When you're involved with someone sexually, it hurts if you break up, it's a much more painful thing, because there are consequences with getting that intimate with someone.' They can really relate to that.

We were talking about this in a staff get together the other day, and one of the staff went, 'Sex isn't as important as we think.' I do know what he means, but it wasn't the right way to express it and I was furious! Partly because it was a man, and I think many men still don't quite get how sex is experienced by women. But also because I think it's really important that we maintain the sense that, yes, the very best way to live according to God is for your sexual relationship to be within a marriage, and we're not afraid to preach that, even though it goes against the grain of today's society. Yet, we're also not afraid to say, you know what, sex isn't actually the biggest deal for God. The biggest deal for God is that he loves you and forgives you and wants you to be in relationship with him.

We had a health professional in to do some sex education the other day, and I was really disappointed that she didn't talk about abstinence being an option. It's so important to give young people that possibility – especially girls – to say, 'You don't have to do it, you know?'

Nobody here who makes the commitment to save sex for marriage does that because it's what's expected, or because it's what other people do. They don't do it lightly. Where any of our young people have made that commitment, it's totally because they can see for themselves that it's right and believe it is right.

So I'm dead proud of Abbi. If you teach a young girl to have self esteem and when her boyfriend says let's have sex, she has the confidence to say, 'No, I'm not ready,' – that's a massive success. That's a blessing from God.

I was thinking what I'd really like is to be a girls' support worker. I would do something like the Academy with the young girls in the area, meeting their emotional and practical needs. It seems that no one teaches these girls how to be women. They are not taught about self esteem or confidence. Also, they haven't got a clue about practical things like budgeting, finances, nutrition, cleaning, child health, family dynamics, all those things. I'm not trying to define a woman as a housewife – but they don't know how to do those things and yet a lot of them go off and have children very early without any of that knowledge.

I'd like to establish a non residential home where they can come during the day and get counselling support, meet their practical needs as far as teaching them to budget, cook and clean and manage a household, and also to look at their training needs – do their computer courses and their GCSEs. Then it would meet their needs now, but also give them skills for the future. It would be a really good thing.

I mean, it wouldn't necessarily be in Bradford – it could be anywhere.

Note

1 See www.everychildmatters.gov.uk/teenagepregnancy/

14

Friend or Foe?

Niki's diary, 21 November 2005

I dropped a bit of a bombshell at the Monday meeting this morning. Julie had been on my mind the whole weekend. I don't know if I'm becoming too involved, but it's really starting to get to me. I know she is getting hurt, and yet there doesn't seem to be anything I can do about it. We sat down for the staff meeting and I said, 'Can I pray for someone to die?' and there was silence.

I just said, 'Can I pray for someone to die – for God to take away the person who is hurting one of our young people? Can I just ask God to completely take him out of the equation, because you know then that young person's life will get better?' I was surprised that I didn't lose it and cry, but I think I was so angry and desperate that I was quite cold about it. Some of them were cross, and said, 'Niki, that's really wrong, that's unacceptable, because even the worst people get a second chance.' But I think they knew where I was coming from at least.

Yan knew. I haven't told him the situation, but he could see how I felt about it. He asked if the young person's mum was around, and when I said yes, he and I talked about going round to see her – not to tell her the situation, but just have a chat with her, maybe even pray with her. So we are going to find a time when we can do that, and that's definitely a positive thing. But overall, I didn't get an answer, really. I don't even know how to pray, I just keep asking God questions.

> Our Father in heaven,
> No Dad on earth.
> What do I pray Lord, what do I say?
> Bruises and insults
> And no way out.
> What do I say Lord, what do I pray?

I really needed some support and a chance to talk things through with someone, so on Sunday I was explaining Julie's situation to a girl I've chatted to a few times, at this church I've been going to. I changed all the details, and made it into a hypothetical scenario – sort of saying, what would you do if . . ., and she said, 'If that was happening, then you would need to get that girl in a place where she can forgive.'

I couldn't believe it. I just said, 'No, that's not it.' Forgive the person in her own household who claims to be protecting her, but instead is beating her up? Forgive while that's still happening, while there's no way out of it? I just know that's unrealistic, and I think God is so much more gracious than that. That's not the answer to it. God understands what people are like.

I mean, Julie is well aware that in five years' time, if he's not part of their life any more, that she might be challenged to forgive and she will. But I think we make the Bible a set of rules in that it says forgive, you'd better forgive now and no understanding is available. That's not right. I don't think God's expecting that right now. Surely, God wants to save her first?

The thing is, people talk about it like they know, but I just don't think they're in the position where they actually have to love the unlovable. And I don't mean kids that are from a difficult background, I mean the people that are hurting those kids. They're not in that position. So they are happy to say that someone else should forgive, but they have no concept of what they would be like in that situation. I wouldn't mind if they said – 'I don't really understand the context you work in, so explain it to me' – but they don't, they just tell you a load of completely unhelpful stuff that's only relevant in their own sphere of life. I'd much rather be open about it and say, actually I have problems with loving this person because . . . ., and work it through, being honest, rather than giving some kind of pat answer that just pushes the problem back on the person who's getting hurt in the first place.

I think she was surprised to see how angry I started to get while we were talking, but I'm part of Julie's life now. I'm involved. In fact, I have become vulnerable about it, and that's dangerous in a way because you can end up getting hurt yourself. But then, I think Jesus got involved. He definitely got hurt.

Yan

It's scary how alone we feel doing this work. We're supposed to be part of the great big family of God, and one of God's most important commissions is to preach good news to the poor, but most of the time the workers here feel like they're not understood, not appreciated, certainly not supported by their churches. I hate to say that but it's true.

I think we are completely out on a limb – I really do. I don't say that because I think no one else is doing the kind of work we do, or even because Bradford is a particularly bad area. It's not. There are lots of people around the UK doing the kind of work we do, with the kind of people we serve. Many of them are doing it in harsher or more dangerous environments than we are. But everyone we've spoken to in this kind of project feels like they're working in isolation.

It feels like the wider church within this country almost doesn't acknowledge us. I can't believe it's an intentional thing, because so many people in the church care about young men and women, and want to reach out to the poor. I guess the problem is the church has fundamentally failed to make a connection between the desire to reach out to the poor and the realities of what it means to be out there, reaching.

We went up to Carlisle once to visit the staff of a project working with young people suffering similar levels of deprivation. We'd met them at a youth conference, and we seemed to have a bit in common so we thought we'd go up and see what we could learn from them. We arrived, they gave us a cup of tea, and then we just started talking to these men and women who were doing the same kind of work as us. There was an incredible sense of relief and release. It was like the best therapy session ever, like coming home and being among family again.

When we said, 'It's hard to see someone come to faith and then be dragged down again because of the drug problems in their environment,' they would nod their heads and know what we meant. They would say, 'We feel out on a limb,' and we would go, 'We feel out on a limb, too!' We would say, 'All the resources we can find are irrelevant to us,' and they would go, 'All the resources we can find are irrelevant to us, too!' It was almost funny in the end – it was like falling in love or something. But afterwards, you think, wow – how tragic that a normal conversation with a few people who understand our work and our challenges is such a novelty that it moves us to that extent.

When we were making the transition to e:merge, setting up as a charitable company, Diarmuid had the task of writing our constitution. We wanted to put in an ethos statement, trying to describe the belief systems our work springs from. He felt it was important to create something that was actually going to be useful and relevant, and could be understood by people who weren't Christians – after all, nearly all our funding sources are secular. How could we use phrases like 'the kingdom of God' to explain how we would use their grants?

So Diarmuid started with the Faithworks[1] template and worked on it until he had something that we were happy with and could be meaningful in explaining our beliefs to others we would work with. He sent it to our lawyer for approval, and when she read it she phoned him to ask, 'What kind of Christians are you? Are you liberal?' Diarmuid couldn't believe it! He said, 'No, we're just using different words – trying to write in a way that people can understand.'

I'm not saying we've found the perfect words – the statement still has the word 'ontological' in the last sentence – but it's depressing how extraordinary Christians find it when you try and communicate in a way that people outside the church might understand.

Within the church, there has been a lack of recognition that youth work is a professional job, which still lingers in places and can be hard on our staff. Many people within the church have, at some point in their lives, helped out with a youth group, and that is now their understanding of what we do, all day every day. They've no concept of the kind of skills we use in terms of facilitation, communication, liaising with other agencies, defusing conflict, creating resources, any of that. A lot of people seem to think we are just messing about with kids. So we find we are justifying ourselves all the time, which we shouldn't need to do, and it gets tiring.

We are desperate for people to understand even just a little bit of what we do and how we do it. Why we can't do the things you would do in a classroom full of attentive, academic, comfortably-off children, or a church full of happy youth group members. We need people to say, 'Sure, we don't understand everything of what you do, but we can see that you know the young people you work with, and that you are doing God's work, so we are going to seek to understand what that work entails. And we're going to suspend our judgement and preconceptions until we really get it.'

Niki's diary, 27 November 2005

I'm still finding it hard to settle into a church, especially since that conversation last weekend. I feel like the church doesn't recognise or understand the environment I work in, which is really ironic because I work in a Christian project! I've tried out a few churches around Bradford now, and it feels like for most of them, the Christian life is still, 'we have to love everyone and no one's allowed to smoke'. Mission is working with African orphans, youth work is hanging out with the kids of people in church, and what I do doesn't seem to fit with any of that.

It's not that people are being difficult or purposely cold shouldering me or anything like that, it's just they ask me what I do and as I'm explaining it, you see them start to clock off. They stop getting it.

I suppose in the absence of belonging to a church family, it's the young people themselves who have become my community. But I could really do with some outside support and understanding. There are some really faithful people at my old home church still praying for me regularly and writing to me, and I don't know whether they realise just how precious that is. It's an absolute lifeline. But I would be stronger still if there was a church community supporting me here, too.

Yan

It's not just the church, it's even some sections of Christian youth ministry. At a large youth event she once went to, Sharon was at a talk about some new material that was being launched for youth ministry. The guy was doing a presentation about how they had designed the material, how it could be used, how they had tested it with various different youth groups during its development. They mentioned that they had piloted it in twenty-eight different places. It was a good number of places, and Sharon was impressed that they had done that degree of research and preparatory work. She asked the guy, 'How many of those pilots were in what you would call urban priority areas?'

He sort of stuttered and seemed to be on the back foot, but he said, out of all of that number of pilots, they had managed to pilot it in potentially three of what they might call urban priority areas. So Sharon asked, 'And what was their response to the material, in those three areas?' The guy appeared to become even more defensive, like this wasn't really what he wanted to talk about. He said, 'Well, you know, you have to understand that using material in an urban context like that – an inner-city context – is different. Those areas are really hard, and it's very difficult to have any material that would work in those areas. However, when we piloted it, the people in those areas said they were able to use *aspects* of it.'

So Sharon got hold of the material to have a look at. It was good material, beautifully packaged and presented, but the only 'aspects' of it that she felt she would be able to use were things like video clips, which we had been using for ages anyway. The rest of it was material that required a certain level of educational achievement among the young people, and was very much geared to a compliant, attentive, enthusiastic youth audience. You can't use that here.

The fact is, most of the money available for Christian youth work is within churches in more wealthy areas. Their members have money, so they can employ a youth worker, and they can buy resources – and because of that spending power, publishers produce resources that are attractive to them. There are a lot of urban inner-city churches that can't afford a youth worker, and who also need a higher ratio of workers to kids because they are reaching the communities around them. So in those cases – and this is what our project was like for many years at the beginning – what you've got is a large body of volunteers trying to run youth clubs or detached projects with very little professional or financial support. They can't afford to buy resources, and they work so hard that they haven't got the time to develop material either, so they're caught in a catch-22 and it's very hard work.

Sharon went away from that session and back to her tent deeply frustrated, thinking that there are thousands and thousands of young people in the inner cities of this country and there are workers that are working so hard to try and reach them but there aren't any resources out there to give them a little bit of help.

Niki's diary, 28 November 2005

Saw an article in a Christian magazine today. It was all about evangelism and went on about how it was a really good idea to give kids books to read as a way of telling them about God. I was really cross! I wrote to the feedback guy and just said, 'No, you can't – a lot of our kids don't read.' And there was another bit where it said, 'Get the young people to discuss such and such with their families,' and I just thought, 'Yeah, in between getting bottles chucked at them.' They just don't get it.

I wrote, 'Please come and visit us. Please come and see what it is we do because I don't think you understand where we're at and why we know these young people will not read a book if we hand it to them and might not have had an actual sober conversation with their parents in years.' I was really cross with the article because it showed there was an underlying assumption that all their kids loved reading, had sorted families and were going to get A stars. Well, most of ours don't and aren't, and it's not acceptable that a national youth magazine doesn't even think to acknowledge that.

I bet he won't come.

Note

1   See www.faithworks.info

15

Support the Workers, Punish the Wicked

Niki's diary, 29 November 2005

Diarmuid called a meeting of all the staff this morning. I'd thought he had looked a bit worried the last couple of weeks, and basically the funding situation for the project has suddenly got really serious. He asked us all to pray that we would get the funding he is negotiating with the West Yorkshire Social Enterprise Link. He said he is hopeful that it will be OK, but he needs the right decision. John asked what would happen if we didn't get it, and Diarmuid just went, 'Well, God will provide.'

Yan

We developed a new resource last year, partly as a response to the lack of relevant materials for our young people. It's a DVD called *Play Paws* and it has games on it that can be used as icebreakers with young people who do not necessarily have the confidence to jump in and participate in traditional group icebreakers. Rather than something paper-based which reminds them of school, or something where they have to participate physically in front of the others, it's all on DVD, and can be played by two people or larger groups.[1] The DVD features a panda character which John dreamed up, called Paws, whose favourite hobbies are playing ping pong and spotting celebrities (John has weird dreams!). So it draws very much on celebrity culture, and the kinds of thing that young people talk about. It's relevant.

John basically started developing *Play Paws* out of pure frustration. He had picked up a book which claimed to be the 'World's Best Icebreakers', but was full of awful ideas like getting all the young people to pull off their socks and see whose were the smelliest, and things like that. There's nothing wrong with being cheesy – *Play Paws* has plenty of cheese – but to have credibility with young people, you have to know how cheesy you are being! You have to do it deliberately. That's kind of where a lot of church youth groups are still stuck in the eighties. We really need to get past *Multi-Coloured Swap Shop* and start presenting work in a way that rivals secular popular culture in its appeal, relevance and style. It's no good trying to win young people for the Lord through resources that make us look like we haven't watched any television for thirty years.

Play Paws has no faith-based content, because it's all about the icebreaker – the setting up of the session. It's set up in such a way that includes the young people quickly, establishing a sense that we understand their world and can relate to the things that they relate to. That's such an important base to have, and yet we have been criticised when we have presented *Play Paws* to people because it doesn't have specifically 'spiritual' content. In fact, when John was presenting the DVD at youth work events, people would often ask him, 'What have these games got to do with the Bible?' He would reply, 'Nothing.' Then they would ask, 'Well, what's the point of it then?' John would explain that the point of it was to enable the young people to relax at the beginning of a session, and for them to have fun. He would point out that if young people were relaxed, engaged and having fun, they were more likely to be receptive to whatever was going to be said or taught later in the session. He would also explain that we don't see why letting young people enjoy themselves and have a laugh together shouldn't qualify as 'spiritual' content. At that point, many people just walked away.

However, despite this kind of reaction from a vocal minority, for e:merge, the *Play Paws* project was exciting, and we know it has been used by lots of other youth work projects and organisations really successfully.

The other thing you can do is try and make sure that your organisation is as supportive as possible. If our staff are not necessarily understood in their church environment, or even by other people in youth work, then let's make sure we give them all the care and strength we can when they're at work.

I didn't really think much about the staff structures at e:merge until we got Diarmuid on board. For so long, the project consisted of a couple of staff – Sharon and myself – and a load of volunteers from the church so we didn't think about salaries or terms and conditions or staff welfare very much. Also, I am the sort of person who is so focused on the young people, on what they need, on how they are doing, that I can forget to look out for the people on the staff.

Sharon and I are so used to working and living together – we will automatically pray together all the time about the things going on with the young people. We come home and talk about e:merge, and this helps when there are issues we need to get off our chest. When the project gets larger, you can't assume that everyone has that kind of support. With Niki, given that she is single, she doesn't have anybody that she can go home and pray with who's really concerned about the same issues as her, or how she's feeling about the young people that she's working with. Not only that, but she also came to Bradford from living elsewhere, so she in a sense has more than one barrier to overcome. She has had to build up her friendships and her church networks from scratch. When you think Sharon and I have been doing that for twelve years, you realise how hard it will be for people arriving in their first year or so.

We are aware that for the people who are single and have moved here to work with e:merge there are excruciatingly difficult and lonely times – whether they are women or men. How much that is about singleness, and how much it is made more raw by working in a harsh environment I don't know, and in a way, that's not relevant. The point is that it's important to recognise how hard it is. There are times when we start to think that it is not right to expect single people from outside the area to come and work here. However, if we had a policy like that, we would never have had Niki – or Diarmuid for that matter. It is something we still grapple with.

e:merge cannot sort out the whole issue for its single staff, or in any way compensate for it, but at least we can make sure that we recognise the sacrifice Niki has made to be here, and try and see that she is treated well by the organisation. We need to have some pastoral structures in place that ensure she can go and talk to someone when necessary – and we also need to have the practical and financial supports in place, too.

Niki's diary, 2 December 2005

I really want to do a counselling diploma course I've seen run by a local college, but it starts next October and lasts for 2 years. I want to get proper, professional counselling skills because there's a real need for them but I don't know if I can face signing up for it because basically, if I do, then I have to stay at e:merge another two and a half years. In my heart, I really want to do the course because it will help with my work, but there's a kind of panic that rises in me at the thought of committing for that long.

A lot of the young people acknowledge that they need counselling, and want to be counselled,[2] but they will not go and see an independent counsellor. They say, 'Why on earth would I go and tell stuff to someone I don't know?' As adults, we can see that it can be beneficial to see a trained professional, and someone who is essentially a stranger, but these young people can't do that – they want relationship. They might well mistrust 'professionals' from experiences they've had with teachers or social workers or the police. They want someone they know because it's so vital to them that they open up to somebody trustworthy. So they already come to me knowing that they need and want counselling, and if they're coming to me for that, I need to be more skilled. It's either that or they just don't get help, because there's no way they're going to go somewhere else for it.

Yan

We have met some fantastic people and worked with great organisations in Bradford who have understood many aspects of what we are trying to do. Within the Academy, we worked with a local jobs brokerage organisation, whose staff came in and set up mock interviews for the students. They gave them interviewing practice and helped them put their CVs together. They understood the small but vital steps we needed to help the students make in order to be ready for work. Doing it in this way, rather than through pure classroom teaching, made it so much more realistic, and the young people – many of whom had never had an interview or written a CV before – appreciated it enormously.

There are other organisations without whose support we would never have got this far. The people who supported our applications to the European Social Fund (ESF), the European Regional Development Fund (EDRF) and Neighbourhood Renewal Fund were fantastic – truly understanding e:merge's vision, and translating that with us into successful funding bids. These people have supported us because they see that what we do is of value and is making a difference in the life of this community and its people. We are so grateful for all these positive relationships, yet we also long to be more understood and embraced by the church in its wider sense. We can't help feeling disappointed when we are doing God's work because some of the people we most want to partner with seem doubtful about the value of what we do.

There are many exceptions though, of course. We now look out more actively for opportunities to link up with other organisations who have the same kind of ethos as us. It isn't always easy, because you can only do it with organisations who share enough of the same vision for it to be meaningful to work together and not compromise your beliefs, but there is a lot you can do. On the practical side, you do have to be prepared to compromise, because inevitably you lose a bit of your organisation's control, and you have to be open to new ways of doing things. But we are open to that because we can see that when people and organisations of like mind get together, it means excellent provision for the young people.

Our biggest struggle has always been creating an environment for our young people where they can express and experience faith in a way that is meaningful to them. Attaching it to the local Sunday morning service just doesn't work, for lots of reasons, nor does taking the young people off to an unfamiliar building, outside the community. We have run the youth congregation since very early on in the project and in 1997 we started youth cells. We got to the point where we had about thirty or forty young people coming. Some were Christians and some not, and there were varying degrees of participation. Some would come every week and stand near the front and sing and pray and everything. Others would only come from time to time, and when they came, they would sit at the edges with their arms folded, and when we broke into the smaller cell groups, they would sit and say nothing. It was a good thing, but we knew it was always some way off its potential. Also, we had this lovely big hall, and with those numbers, we kind of rattled.

There was also an issue with the age range. We were trying to cater for young people right through about eleven years old to eighteen and above, and there's a massive difference between an eleven-year-old boy and an eighteen-year-old young woman, for example. We were worried that by trying to put on something that was relevant to all of them we would actually end up having something spread so thinly that it didn't meet any of their needs.

I had a feeling that in Bradford 4 – this side of Bradford, but wider than our immediate catchment – we should maybe look at teaming up. We talked to about five different Christian organisations whose work we already knew and respected. We discussed the possibility of creating a renewed, merged Friday night youth congregation with them, and we gave time for all of them to pray and consider it and get back to us to see what they thought.

Out of the five organisations, four of them said no. They wanted to retain their existing work. And I think it was really important on lots of levels that we took it slowly and were very open about whether they wanted to come in on it or not. It means we have created and kept respect between the organisations, not getting resentful or competitive – above all, we would hate for any of the organisations' own work to suffer because of a badly-thought-through joint venture.

However, the fifth organisation was called Youth Base, and they decided that yes, they wanted to work together with us. They are people we have known and worked with for a long time. Their work and ours have a lot of similar characteristics and our journeys have been similar. We had previously joined up for some cell leader training and summer events.

We started together carefully and quite gradually. I think both organisations were worried they might spoil what they already had, and that would have been disastrous. We worked out the different responsibilities, and the way it would all happen, then we relaunched it together, and suddenly it created a whole new momentum.

On a very practical level, it means the tasks of devising, preparing and leading the sessions are shared out between a larger number of people, which takes a bit of pressure off all of us. We have also started doing cells a bit differently – so one week we'll all meet together in the e:merge building, and the next week, we'll have four clusters of cell groups meeting together in four locations – one of which is e:merge. We couldn't have done that with the staff levels we had on our own. It means there's more opportunity for really good work in small groups.

Beyond those specific things, I think the atmosphere that has been created by working together has been amazing. I really think God has blessed our coming together. You can't force that, and it's disastrous to make people or organisations work together on something if they don't have a shared vision for it, but we really did. Today, we have eighty or ninety young people coming on any given Friday night, and over the first 12 months, more than 200 young people had attended. It was named 'Xstream' by the young people, and it had a whole new energy and momentum. From there, we tried to kind of sit back and help things happen naturally where we could, because this momentum had been established. Slowly but surely, we've seen more young people actually experiencing and participating. A band has formed, so young people lead their own worship. We have young people manning the sound desk and the audio-visuals. There's so much more of a buzz than there used to be, and there's this great number of young people who are open to God and who are learning about God. There's a lot of ownership from among the young people and it's creating a very positive experience. It means, with that number, that we can try new things – and the social time at the end, which is really important for young people, is more dynamic, too. Since the start, two other Bradford 4 youth projects have also become involved in the youth congregation.

The other thing that's come quite naturally because of the numbers is that suddenly it doesn't matter whether you're eleven or eighteen on a Friday night, because there's a critical mass. So the whole thing about how we meet all of their needs has stopped being such a pressing problem. I won't say it's solved, but because there are so many people, they all just join in as far and in whatever way they can. Also, the fact that we are doing more cell-group work is addressing that, because by their nature small groups mean people can help each other with their individual needs more easily.

A few years ago, there was a lot of debate across the UK about whether youth church is the right model – whether it's right to have a separate youth congregation from a mainstream church congregation – and we don't pretend to have the answer to that universally. All we can do is what is right in this context, for these young people, and when it's not right any more, we'll stop doing it. Our thirst is to make Christ accessible to young people here – and we will do that in any way that works.

We don't see Friday night congregation as 'church'. Church is everything we do. Drop-ins, the Academy, Xposure – all this is church, because church is simply the way that people with faith interact and encourage each other, and bless people around them. There's no separation.

As well as attending Xstream, we still encourage young people who are Christians to go to a local church community where they can and they are open to that. Xstream doesn't rival church. It creates hope that more young people will find their way into an adult congregation, because they have a kind of halfway house – a place they can come and meet God and worship him, but not feel they are in an alien or pressured environment. They will stick around and be more committed here at Xstream, and one day as they get older, or just more mature and spiritually hungry, they may well take the step to a wider church congregation, because they have been in an environment where their faith has been able to grow.

The merger has had its ups and downs – there have been relationships to work out between Youth Base and ourselves. There has been the issue of two organisations with separate identities working together and having to be prepared to put those identities aside to form a shared identity. Now that we are exploring other, newer ways of working even more closely together, we all know that there will be times when there is friction, but I think if the vision you share is strong enough, and if both organisations come down to the bottom line of caring for young people and wanting to see their lives improved, then it can really work.

We didn't rush or presume anything, and we stayed faithful to our core business without being obstinate, and it has been a real success. I think that if you are in an urban area, this is one of the ways to go – to really decide that you're going to team up with somebody else. You're going to put aside your own minor agendas where you have to, and you're going to do this work.

Niki's diary, 5 December 2005

I had a hilarious conversation with Paul this afternoon. He's been a Christian a couple of years, and he came up to me at drop in and said, 'Niki, can I ask you a question?'

'Yes, of course you can.'

'Why does God want to punish the wicked?'

'What?'

'We did a psalm at Xstream on Friday, and it said, "God will punish the wicked". But why would God want to punish the wicked?'

'Er, because they're wicked.'

'Exactly. So why punish them?'

'Well, because God is fair and at the end of the day, if people go on being wicked and don't change their behaviours . . .' Then it occurred to me. 'Oh, Paul, it doesn't mean wicked as in, "That's wikkid, man!" – it's not a good thing.'

'What is it then?'

'It means wicked, as in really bad, cruel, unkind.'

'Oh, right. Oh, OK, good. That makes sense now. Ta Niki!'

Note

1   *Play Paws* is available to buy at Wesley Owen and other Christian bookshops. See www.playpaws.co.uk

2   In the DfES's 'Every child matters' consultation, more than 50 per cent of young people questioned said that they wanted counselling available in schools – many more than said they wanted youth centres or food.

16

Did Jesus Go Home On Time?

Niki's diary, 6 December 2005

It looks like it might not even be up to me any more whether or not I stay beyond my one year. Diarmuid sat us down again today and said, 'Guys, I have to tell you, if we don't get that WYSE Link funding, then there is a serious probability that this whole project will have to be shut down.'

It's not that it's a load of money, apparently, but it's reliable funding right now when we really need it, for what we really need to do. It was quite sobering, because you kind of tick along thinking everything is fine, and then suddenly you're staring at the very real possibility of not doing this work any more. It was weird and really scary. Funnily enough, I wasn't scared about losing my job, because basically, I will always be able to find some kind of work, but I was absolutely terrified to think about what would happen to some of our young people if this project shut down.

We've got a girl on work experience this week, and she has started asking loads of questions about God. We were making Christmas cards at drop in yesterday, sitting round with sparkly card and scissors and stuff. She was asking, 'Why should I be a Christian and how do you know God's there?' I opened my mouth to respond to her, but suddenly, some of the young people were around, and one of them went, 'You know God's real because you can feel him and it feels all tingly,' and then another lad went, 'Well yeah, but Caz says that about hot chocolate!' And then another said, 'Yeah, but you know you're forgiven, and it makes it a bit easier not to make stupid choices.'

It was a really serious conversation, at drop in, and all these kids, these tough characters, who I had never heard talk about God or in any way express their faith, they were testifying to her. They were explaining how it was for them, what God's done and who he is for them. I felt really chuffed but humbled as well. It's like, you think, ugh, nothing is happening – I've been here for months and months yet I'm not making any difference. And suddenly a little thing like this happens, and it's like – hey, where did that come from? Because the kids don't make a big deal about rushing into things, or telling everyone they've 'become a Christian', there isn't necessarily a single defining moment, but every little seed you plant can have an impact, somehow it all makes a difference. It stays there, and one day, maybe months or years later, and sometimes when you least expect it, suddenly you see this little green leaf appear, and it's like – oh my goodness, it's alive! It's growing!

Then today to be told it might all be over, it was absolutely gutting. We are all praying, so hard.

Yan

I think e:merge is in an interesting and quite unusual position. We started off – twelve years ago now – as a small project that was wholly part of a church. It was the youth work ministry of St Mary's Church in Bradford. Now we are a charitable trust independent from any church or Christian organisation, and we are run much more along business principles. Yet we still have a completely Christian ethos and that is set out in our business plans and mission statement.

Many churches have a wonderful heart to reach out to their community, and they do wonderful work. Ironically, the problems start when the work flourishes and grows. What happened in our case was that the people overseeing our work, with authority for it, were being forced to tackle uncharted legal and financial waters because of our growth. In any sector, a small organisation functions in completely different ways to a large one, and often your policies and structures need to be more robust and formalised when you are larger. For us, we had a project that was growing, and becoming more professionally framed, but a structure that was still set up to oversee a small, church-based work. It started to become contradictory and required a change.

It was no disrespect to the people at St Mary's, because their hearts were in the right place, and it was due to their work that the project was so successful. It had started as a small thing, working with parents and toddlers and the elderly and then youth, but then it had grown on the youth side disproportionately. If something grows like that, there comes a point when the church either needs to let it go and be independent, or it has to be reigned in and made smaller again. None of us wanted to reign in the youth work, so the church had to let it go.

I wouldn't say in every single instance going independent is the best approach, but one of the things that swung it for us was that the funding sources that churches normally apply to were drying up. Once we started having to look for larger pots of money like European funding streams, for example, we had to demonstrate much more developed systems of governance and monitoring, and that was just not possible the way we were set up within the church. The funders need to know exactly what you are doing with the money – so you need good business planning and monitoring systems to demonstrate that the money will be managed effectively. You have to show, quite rightly, that you are dealing properly with your staff and have the right policies in place for running your work effectively. Almost all of our funding now comes from outside sources that we have to apply for. Much less of our income comes from private donations than it used to.

One of the lessons that we would draw from this experience is that the church at every level and in all denominations needs to ensure that its leaders are trained in people management. Most vicars or pastors of churches are going to be managing staff – whether it's one voluntary secretary and some home group leaders or a group of volunteer youth workers or employed staff in a range of jobs. Many youth workers in churches or Christian projects will be leading and managing other youth workers, whether voluntary or employed. Yet there seems to be insufficient training and preparation given for the vital professional ability to manage and lead people. We quite rightly recruit visionary, passionate leaders, but overlook the fact that they also need to be able to properly supervise staff – therefore they are not equipped with the professional expertise to do so.

Once we had decided to go down the road of becoming a separate entity, it gave us the opportunity to re-assess who we were. It gave us the opportunity to start afresh, with a new, corporate image and we interviewed for directors. We went and got the people we needed with the skill sets the project required: someone with legal skills, someone who knew about property, someone with financial know-how and so on. We were able to tailor what we needed in terms of leadership and steering, to get e:merge off on the right foot.

I think one of the things that we have found we can do better as an independent organisation compared to being a church-based project is stay fresh and relevant. When you're running on external funding, and reporting to a board of directors on a regular basis, you don't keep doing the same things because you've been doing them so long. You question them, and ask, 'Is this still the best way to do it? Are we still making the most of the funding we receive? Because if not, we need to change.'

I don't have a firm view about which is better – church-based or independent youth projects. There are risks and benefits both ways, and the reality is that a huge proportion of projects that come out of the church lose their Christian dynamic within the first generation of leadership changes. They become secular projects.

Some people will say there's nothing wrong with that in a sense – if the project is still achieving its objectives – but actually, it's a big deal if your objectives include caring for people's spiritual needs. You've lost that identity.

So I wouldn't recommend it to everyone, but I definitely think it was the right thing for us to do at that particular time. As an independent project, we can focus on our core business of improving lives for young people around Bradford 4. It is easier for us to network with statutory and other voluntary agencies, because people can see we're a professional outfit with a board of directors, proper policies and good forward planning. We use all that to make sure we serve the young people of Bradford 4 in the best possible way.

Niki's diary, 8 December 2005

Julie told me she's mean to people and gives them a hard time because she doesn't want them to get close to her. She doesn't want them to get close to her because she is scared they will let her down and hurt her. It's obvious really, now she's explained it. She said the fact that I kept going and kept loving her and kept being kind, kept inviting her to stuff and wouldn't give up on her, it all made her see that I wasn't going to go away and that she could trust me.

Even though her problems are nowhere near at an end, it was brilliant to hear her have the understanding and words to explain that – and the confidence. Incredible really that her being mean was just testing me to see how far she could push me and whether or not I'd keep coming back.

Yan

We are a Christian project driven by faith and mission, and we are also an independent, professional project driven by business objectives and good practice. We try and get the best of both worlds, and I think that is possible.

Our staff give more than 100 per cent – I know they see this as a lifestyle rather than purely a job. At the same time, we make sure that as employees they are treated in a way that is appropriate for skilled professionals.

Early on, I remember Diarmuid saying to me, 'If you're working for God, do you not think he's the best employer, so therefore should your agency not reflect that?' I hadn't thought about it that way before.

All our staff are on a pension scheme. We have proper annual leave arrangements that we ensure our staff take. We gave Niki a relocation allowance – it's not huge, but it helps, and it says to our staff, 'we recognise the facts of life and the costs of moving – and we honour your decision to move here'. We offer a salary package, including pension, which is in line with local, national and EU recommendations – in fact it's now just above the national average for youth work. Part of the reason for that is that we need to recognise that the difficulties and hardships associated with working in this project mean our recruitment and retention is more difficult than elsewhere. In terms of pure business sense, recruitment isn't cheap – so spending on training, allowances and decent terms and conditions is a small investment for loyalty and retention, not to mention the skills and quality of provision.

All our staff get a minimum of £500 worth of training a year. Not just as a kind of gift or treat, but because they must be equipped properly with the skills and abilities to do this job well – both for themselves, and for the young people we serve. Also, within the training, we recognise not just what their needs are in terms of working for e:merge, but also what their own vision is for their life – building into that. We can't tell how long people are going to be here – a year, five years, ten years? Who knows? But I think once staff are committed here, we're interested not only in the distance they'll travel personally and professionally while they're with us but also what they will take with them wherever they go next. We want them to leave better equipped personally and professionally to do the work God has for them.

There's been a history of Christians working for little money, without leave or breaks and with very little support or structure around them in mission-focused jobs which are very stressful. For many of the people here, because we believe in what we are doing, we are prepared to do it for little money, but the fact is, God has enabled us as communities and churches and a national and international church to have the resources to support each other. No mission worker should be getting completely burned out because they are simply not being managed properly or supported adequately. That's ridiculous. And yes, there will always be a need for volunteer workers, but actually, God has made funds available through his church and through all sorts of charitable avenues that with the right skills and organisation we can draw on. There is nothing to show off about by being on a low wage if actually you don't need to be.

When Diarmuid arrived here, I think he was quite shocked at how we were running the project. We were all the youth workers – the passionate, missionary side of the work. Nobody here was a bureaucrat, an organiser or administrator. So there was a huge gap. And he was quite shocked that we were working for such low pay. It took him six months to get the measure of the project, and then to start campaigning to get our salaries up to proper levels. There were issues we needed to sort out about having the right people in the right jobs, and we also had the opportunity to be able to plan staff resources better, according to the funds we had coming in. Our staff turnover rate is now comparable to, if not better than, that in the secular youth work sector, and I think that reflects to a large degree the way we treat our staff, as well as the work we do.

We all now desire to go on making e:merge an excellent organisation. It's not for its own sake, it's because that is how we will best serve the young people. If e:merge becomes recognised as an employer of choice, for example we will attract the best youth workers to work for us, which means they'll get the best out of the young people that we have. If we get our structures and business planning right, we are more likely to attract more significant and sustainable funding, which means a more secure organisation, which again, filters down to the young people, because we're not living hand-to-mouth so we can channel our energies into serving them. Excellence also starts to mean that we have a voice on the national agenda. So, as we have grown as a professional organisation, we have made connections and networks not only in Yorkshire but round the country. We can share our experience and support others in getting excellent results for young people.

I definitely recognise that as we strive for excellence in both our Christian commitment and our business focus, we will sometimes get the balance wrong. It can be just as possible to swing too much towards the business side as it is to swing away from it. Our focus is always, 'what difference are we making in the quality of life of the young people we are here for?' So although we don't want to be badly paid, overstressed youth workers with a great heart but no pension, we also don't want to be super-organised youth workers who spend more time in business meetings than with young people. It's something we have to keep an eye on, because at the end of the day, the only reason we operate as an independent, more professional and businesslike organisation is because we believe that is what will give the best service to the young people we work with. Our heart is just the same, and having good business practices is the best way for our heart to get out to the people we want to serve.

Niki's diary, 15 December 2005

It was like a funeral or something in the office this morning. We knew Diarmuid was expecting a call around 10 o'clock about the funding, and no one could bring themselves to do anything at all. I just sat at my desk not able to concentrate on anything. I found myself staring at the books, files and manuals all around the walls – reports about youth work, papers about young people, policies, everything – and I was thinking, 'We'll really need a lot of boxes for those,' and then, 'Oh, I suppose we'll just throw them away.' It was horrible. Then the phone went and although no one was speaking anyway, it kind of went even more silent and you just heard Diarmuid's voice as though it was really, really loud saying, 'Hello?'

into this emptiness. It felt like an absolute age before we heard anything more of the conversation, with just the person on the other end talking, and then suddenly he just said, 'We did?' and then broke into this massive grin, saying, 'Oh my goodness! Thank you! Thank you so much!'

The rest of us literally started leaping up and down with joy while he was still finishing the conversation, but trying to do it quietly and without shouting because we didn't want to sound like a load of monkeys in the background, but oh it was so wonderful! e:merge lives on. What a total relief!

Yan

When Sharon and I arrived here, one of the things that made the most difference to our work was the attitude of the minister at St Mary's. He was so welcoming, so generous, and did not feel like he had to be in total control of everything we did. He allowed us to make mistakes – and made sure we learned from them, and I think that has stood us in very good stead. We felt empowered, and that gave us confidence to really go for it in terms of serving the young people. Leadership is so important, and yet the church seems often to lag behind the world in terms of recognising and emulating good leadership practice. Jesus was the first and ultimate servant leader, and yet Christian leadership can so often be about control and strength rather than service and gentleness. If youth workers are not looked after properly, what message is that giving the young people?

I have always tried to retain that sense of knowing that we will make more mistakes, and that mistakes are not things to fear. If we learn from them, mistakes are positive. I hope that's a key feature of the way I lead e:merge now. Whenever we come back from a session, a trip, a new activity, anything, we constantly critique what we have done, in a very open way. I will say something like, 'I thought the start of that session went well, but we didn't connect enough in the second half – I think I chose the wrong topic to talk about.' The other staff will then agree or disagree or whatever, and we'll discuss what to do differently next time. That makes us a learning organisation and prevents people being scared to take risks. It's not a big deal when something goes wrong – and the more you pick up on the small mistakes, the more you avoid the large ones.

I think sometimes for new staff, the way we constantly and honestly critique our own work can seem quite harsh, but I hope they soon realise that we are interested in doing the best we can, and that's why we question everything, within the confidence of allowing each other and ourselves to make mistakes.

Niki's diary, 20 December 2005

Everything is about relationships, even funding! Yan was saying that the reason we did get the support and funding from WYSE Link isn't because we filled all the forms in correctly (though I'm sure we did!) but actually because the people we have discussed it with there believe in us and in what we are doing. Diarmuid has invested time building relationship with them and e:merge, and that is what paid off.

Now that we've got the funding secured, Diarmuid is trying to get all the staff to write five year plans for their lives. We were taking the mick out of him because it's like, now he knows the money is there, he's going into planning overdrive!! Basically, he's very good at all the things that need to be done professionally, that the rest of us haven't really got much of a clue about, and we laugh at him for it, which is bad really, because he's often right. Every one of us has worked in the kind of project that is all about relating to the young people and then muddling through on the admin side, living hand to mouth and never having any long term strategy – which is not very honourable to God when you think about it. And it's probably the reason why so many church youth projects end up folding. Apparently the average burn out time for a youth worker is three years. Great!

The thing is, the professional structures give you a foundation from which to work and enable you to express your faith more into the work you do. So even when the work is really difficult, at least you know you're getting paid and you're getting a good wage, whereas in the past, my faith has been trusting God in my future, my security, where I'm getting my next pay cheque from – that kind of thing. Here, as long as the project is there, I don't have to worry about my pension and the future, or what'll happen if I get sick, and it frees up my faith to believe for the other things – the more important things – seeing young people's lives change.

Anyway, I gave it a go, because Diarmuid knows what he's talking about, and he said these five year plans would help us all focus on what we want to achieve and how to keep developing ourselves professionally.

Every which way I try and write a five year plan, though, it ends up having a counselling diploma in it, and me staying at e:merge . . . Aaargh!

Yan

Basically, at e:merge you've got a choice. You can guard yourself and keep yourself safe, or you can get involved. I don't think there's a middle way. I don't think there's any question that working here is more than a job. You can call it a vocation, a ministry, a calling, a lifestyle, a mission – whatever. The point is, you can't do it as purely a nine-to-five.

What people don't realise until they come here is that we are Jesus to these kids. They don't have a lot of education. They don't have any previous understanding of what Christianity is. They don't read books – they certainly don't read the Bible. The only experience most of them have of Jesus is us. We are the books that they read. We don't just preach the gospel, we *are* the gospel. It's a massive responsibility and we can't walk out on it.

When Jesus came, he was the ultimate embodiment of what humanity could be – his life was a pattern for us. When I and the people around me know the truth of God being with us, and understand who Jesus is, and try to live that same sense of closeness to God and of love for other people, that is when we can truly become the hope of God to our communities, wherever they are.

So many times in the past, young people have commented about our lives – and that's where they start getting interested in God. I'm not saying that all our project workers have perfect, godly lives all of the time. We don't – of course not. But what happens is, the young people look at our lives and will make comments. When I get things wrong they will challenge me about it, and I can explain that I believe God forgives me, and forgives anyone who admits they have gone wrong, and that I can pick myself up and try again, however many times it takes. When I get things right they will ask me about it, and I can explain the way I live my life, and how that relates to what I believe about Jesus.

Someone asked me what it was that these young people here saw in me and the staff. So I said, 'Let's go and ask them.' We went to where some lads were playing pool and on the Playstation, and they said that the staff are friendly – they are fun, they care, you can talk to them. They ask you if you're OK, and they really want to know. They don't judge you. They make you feel like you're an equal. They go the extra distance.

This is what it's all about for us – creating relationships with the young people. It's only when you've created a relationship in which they feel valued, respected and trusted that we can help them make changes in their lives. What it means for the youth workers is that we are very open to the young people – our lives are that open book – which can be quite scary at first, and quite raw. But it's the only way to do it. Going the extra mile is actually just the first step of the journey.

One of the hardest things is the combination of living God's absolute grace and yet setting a really good example as the youth leader. I want the kids to know that lying and disrespectful behaviour and all those things are absolutely wrong, and not the way God wants us to live. So I must set them an example. At the same time, I must demonstrate the absolute grace of God every time they make a mistake. I must show them that God doesn't give up on them. God wants all of us to completely succeed, and part of that is that he is prepared to forgive and pick us up every time we make a mistake – but equally, it doesn't mean he relaxes his standards. That's part of being Jesus. He always walked in God's ways, and in his humanity, he was absolutely holy. Yet he didn't turn away people who hadn't so far lived up to God's standards in their lives. He didn't wince when a woman came to him who had been caught in adultery. He spoke to her and refused to criticise her. he didn't shun the tax-collector, who was a social pariah, he went and ate a meal with him. He didn't listen to the Pharisees who said, 'your disciples are eating bits of corn on the Sabbath' because he knew what was most important. He accepted people first and foremost, and then after that acceptance he helped them deal with their problems, their sin.

I think as Christians we should all be working to be more like that – more and more holy in our own lives, and more and more accepting before anything else of other people, wherever they're at. In youth work, it's more immediate and crucial, because you are so close to the young people you work with – there are no barriers or social niceties. They need to see the truth through us, before they can start understanding and being open to theology and reading the Bible.

The implication for youth workers is that we need support, too. Vocation is not an excuse to leave people out on their own. We are giving out to the young people here all the time, and we need to be understood and supported from those outside and around us. As a youth worker, having your life constantly on display is tiring. We are not trying to live unbelievable lives – we are real – and we make mistakes and fail like anyone does. We really need support from a church family and from prayer partners and, frankly, just from friends who will come and visit us, talk to us, listen to us and invite us away for the weekend from time to time. When you work in a deprived area and with people who are marginalised, you can become overtaken yourself by those things. Unless we have our spirits lifted by the wider church family, we will become as marginalised as the people we are seeking to help.

Niki's diary, 20 December 2005

I'm going to my parents in Macclesfield for a week and a half over Christmas. I nearly said, 'I'm going home' but that's not home any more. In a funny way, I felt a bit reluctant to leave Bradford. Not because of the place, but because of the people. I know that some people will say I've got too involved – that it's not professional to get too close. And in one way, I am too involved, in the sense that when any of the young people I'm close to is hurting, that hurts me, too. But I can't step out, or be neutral about it, because these are people and they are my friends.

I don't feel like this is my profession. It's more than that. It's my calling. And I think it's possible to be totally professional and also to be a genuine friend. In fact, I don't think you should separate them if you're really trying to be like Jesus. I mean, who knows what I'll be doing in the future – everything might change for me – but for now, for what God is calling me to in the present time, I need to be right here in it, in a very consistent and non hypocritical way. My heart is to live in the community so the kids know where I am. Sure, sometimes I think to myself that I would love a posher house, in a leafier area, just for the attractiveness of the environment. But at the moment, it would be wrong of me to bus in from some lovely, exclusive estate up the road, because the message it would give the young people would be, 'I want to work with you but I don't really want to be part of your life and live near you because I'm above that.' I'm not saying this is what every youth worker has to do. I'm not responsible for everyone else's choices – it's between them and God. And not absolutely everyone here lives in the community, actually. But for me, given the job I have to do for God right now, I need to be here.

I feel very much in this job that I'm an advocate – an advocate is someone who walks alongside, not just walking alongside till 5 o'clock and it's time for me to go. The kids who I've started having some kind of connection with know that if they need me, they can text me. Either you walk alongside someone or you don't. I mean, I'm not stupid – I take my holidays and spend time on my own when I need to recharge. I'm no good to anyone if I work all the hours God sends and finish up exhausting myself. But at the end of the day, how on earth can you expect young people to open up about their lives if you're not willing to give?

Which reminds me, I still haven't done that five year plan . . .

Yan

At the end of the day, I think we all feel very fortunate that we've got the opportunity to be in this place. That's the thing that I keep going back to. Many things about the lifestyle we have chosen are hard, and many things about the way we are perceived by others – including the church – are difficult and frustrating. But when you reckon it up, being here with young people and becoming someone who is a positive influence on their lives is a privilege.

We see God's grace in action here. We see young people becoming more able to deal with and resolve problems because they're experiencing the grace of God. We see people who have made incredibly bad choices, and alongside that, you see God desperate to be generous to them, longing to pour grace out on them. It's an amazing thing to see, when a person starts to realise that the way they have messed up their lives is not permanent, without any possibility of turning round. They have hope, they have forgiveness, they can change. You can't put a value on that. It may be hard, but it's not a hardship.

17

Matthew's Story

Yan

We had a young lad who we worked with for a long time. I worked with him a lot, very closely. He was a drug addict. He was fifteen when we first met him. He would stay over at our house sometimes because his mum needed a break and she would give permission for him to sleep over at our house because then she knew where he was and she knew he was safe. She couldn't always have him stay in her house – there was no father present, just her, and if Matthew was in the house with the mum, he would sometimes rob her blind. When that happened, he would take anything he could – her TV, her iron, anything – to sell for smack. It was a nightmare for her.

She used to call me sometimes, to get me to carry him out of her house for her. If she was going to work or something, and she couldn't leave him in the house, she would call and ask me to please come and get Matthew out of the house. I'd go down and have to pick up Matthew and carry him out of the house. Sometimes he would struggle a bit but then he'd always give in and I would be able to carry him out. He might give me a bit of abuse but not much really, because he knew I loved him, I think. He just knew I cared about him.

He would come to stay at our house, and he had no clothes except for the clothes he stood up in, because if ever he had any extra clothes, he would sell them to buy smack. When he came to us, Sharon would put his shirt in the wash and put it to dry overnight. He would have a shower, have something to eat and go to bed. Often he'd be hurting because he hadn't used recently.

If he couldn't sleep – because you don't sleep very long if you are a user – I used to play games with him. *Tomb Raider* or something like that. We always explained to him that the burglar alarm was on, so he couldn't leave the house without us. That way he knew he couldn't leave suddenly, but apart from that we just had to trust him. We didn't lock anything up, we just trusted him. He never stole from us.

He always wanted to be up and out quite early in the morning. It was a strange contrast. In many ways, he was immaculate. He would get up in the morning, would ask politely to use our iron, would iron his shirt and off he would go.

I often talked to him about God, and on one occasion when we were together, he just said to me, 'I need God. I need somehow to get things sorted.' That was when he was sixteen or seventeen. I sat down with him for some time and answered all his questions as best I could, and explained how Jesus died exactly for people like him – for people who were not sorted. I told him about forgiveness, and the love of God for him, and we prayed together.

After that, he would always say, 'I believe. I believe in Jesus and I know Jesus loves me.' It was wonderful. I knew there was a long way to go to get his life back in any kind of order, but at those times, I knew he knew the love of God.

His mum became a Christian as well. At first, I would go round and when I talked about God she would just say to me, 'I don't need it. Matthew needs it. Tell Matthew.' Then suddenly one year, a couple of weeks before Christmas, she phoned us and asked me, 'Are you going to church this morning?'

'Yeah, I am.'

'Can I come?'

'Yes, that's fine.'

'Will you meet me at the door?'

'Yeah, I'll meet you, I'll make sure I'm there.'

So we met her at the door and she came in and sat through the service. At the end of the service she asked to be prayed with. She received Christ very simply, it was a total conversion and she started to come to church. I remember that first Christmas, her being in church on Christmas Day.

We tried a lot of things with Matthew. We tried to team up with various rehabilitations, we tried taking him off to youth weekends, and referring him to special projects, but he just never made a go of it.

I spoke at his funeral. He had been put in prison, on remand, for stealing again – because it had happened so many times, they wouldn't give him bail. He was on suicide watch and they were actually checking him every fifteen minutes and he still managed to do it. That was terrible – Esther was only about three weeks old when that happened. Ben would have been four years old. Matthew hadn't reached the age of twenty.

His mum really wanted me to speak at his funeral. She didn't want a sermon. She just wanted me to talk about Matthew a bit. The church was full, with people standing all down the side aisles. I talked about God's forgiveness, and his commitment to us, even when we are unfaithful, even when we are too weak to live up to anyone's expectations. I talked about the fact that Matthew had found God and knew him, and now would be close together with him. It was very important to Matthew's mum that he had made that commitment to God – very, very important.

I think you do still wonder, why didn't God just heal him from his drug addiction? But everything's so circular, so interrelated. Everything's such a mess. So even if Jesus had healed the addiction, there's still the lifestyle to be addressed. It's people's lifestyle that really leads them into addiction, and then it's the addiction that leads them into all the other things that go wrong.

Matthew's mum doesn't ask that sort of question. She really understands addiction very well because she lived with it for so long. From her perspective she thinks that not enough is being done in our society, in our communities and by our government to address the causes and effects of addiction.

I wish it were simpler, but it's not. Even if Jesus did come in and miraculously heal Matthew's addiction in a moment, what about the other aspects? What about the lives of those people who impact on Matthew and his choices – would they be miraculously healed, too, of all the issues they have to face? If not, you'd still have the impact of some of Matthew's closest influences still using drugs and committing crimes to fund their habits. And then, if Matthew had a miraculous healing, would he then have had a miraculous character change, too? Are his accommodation circumstances and all the issues in his family going to be miraculously sorted out? No, they're not. It's not that simple, because of all the things that have led someone like Matthew to get into the mess in the first place.

So I could ask those questions – why wasn't he transformed? Why wasn't he healed? But I don't anymore. And I can become frustrated by people who would come in from a different kind of church experience, or have never seen these difficult lives close-up, and would say, 'You didn't have enough faith. Did you try praying for him? Did you try laying hands on him?' That has actually happened – when people have asked, 'But did you pray for him?' I could really take offence with somebody like that. I could say, 'Hang on a minute, we are trying hard for people like Matthew – we have them in our house, we feed them, we listen to them, we counsel them, we link with their families, we speak up for them to the police. Well, sorry if that's not as spiritual as laying on hands for five minutes.'

But you have to protect yourself from being cynical or you will get bitter and twisted and that's no good either. Of course, we prayed for Matthew – we prayed for him often. We also walked with him.

Matthew's mother went and talked to the prison governor after his death, in the prison where Matthew died. She wanted to talk to the governor, and to explain how she felt. She saw a lot of addicts while she was there and she talked to the governor about how if young lads come in with addictions, they really need a lot of support because they're in despair. The governor was in bits. The man was really upset. He was very good with her, and she was able to say what she wanted to say, find out what she wanted to find out, and just in that, there was a tiny bit of peace for her. She believes Matthew has gone to a better place, but he could have had so much more of a life before he went there.

18

The People God Prefers

Niki's diary, 25 January 2006

We were in the car on the way back from town last night, and Abbi was really upset about something. Without me suggesting it, Julie asked, 'Shall I pray for you?' So she did, in the car – just reached over and held Abbi's hand, and prayed, 'God please help her in this situation. Amen.' God really showed up. I could feel Him in the car, like a presence. And when Abbi got out of the car and went off home, Julie said to me, 'I could feel God, he was there.'

She prays a lot for other people, I've discovered, and she kind of knows what's going on. Like, almost freaky – she'll say, such and such is happening to so and so, and it's not because they have told her, she just knows. God reveals it to her. I think things like that really keep her going. I don't know how she copes otherwise.

I can't help but think that something amazing's going to happen in the future for Julie, that God's really going to use her because of the battles that she's got. I'm afraid for her though, a lot of the time.

Yan

Working at e:merge has changed us all I reckon. In some ways it has made people here despondent about the church, because we feel we are misunderstood and not supported enough. But at the same time, it's made us more and more convinced that God's heart is for the poor. This is where God wants to be. God wants to be with those who are broken, who have no voice, who have no hope. Jesus didn't opt for a comfortable life. When he came into the temple in Luke chapter 4, he very clearly stated what he had come to do – to preach good news to the poor, recovery of sight to the blind, to bind up the broken-hearted.

In Luke chapter 4, the Greek word used for 'poor' is 'ptochos'. Its meaning is more than just those who are economically poor. It means people who are marginalised, the disaffected, the hungry, the voiceless, the physically infirm – all those on the fringes of society. You find it right through Scripture. Blessed are the poor in heart, blessed are the meek, blessed are the humble. In the Old Testament, there's the concept of the year of jubilee, where every fifty years, everything would be given back to the original owners so that nobody could become too rich and nobody could become too poor (see Leviticus 25:10–13).

God's heart is overwhelmingly for the poor, in the widest sense of the word 'poor'. I really think that's a fact – the place Jesus and God overwhelmingly want to be is where people are hurting. Sometimes we perceive God as wanting to be with successful people, but actually, I think God's nature as long as this world continues is to automatically go towards the people in pain, the people who have had a rough deal. I actually think God loves poor people best.

Of course, you're talking about the fact that God's love is so enormous that I don't in any way feel unloved just because he loves the poor best. Nevertheless, I think his bias is to the poor, his bias is to the underdog. That might feel uncomfortable to people who have benefited most from the economic and social systems of this world – but tough, it's scriptural.

If Jesus walked into a room full of people, I think he would naturally gravitate towards the people there who were hurting most. In the way that some people would immediately look for the most beautiful people, the richest, the trendiest, the funniest – whoever might make them look good, or show them a good time – Jesus goes towards the people who have the least. I just think that something about his gracious, generous, compassionate nature means that the people most disadvantaged by this world are the ones he most wants to live amongst.

When Jesus came, he was interested in upsetting the social order of society. Not through physical warfare, but by valuing those who were losing out and prizing those who were looked down on. Jesus spent time with richer people, yes, but actually the focus of his ministry was the people on the margins of society – in his day, that meant the tax collectors, the prostitutes, the women, the lepers, the sick, the beggars, the widows and the orphans. The Bible often talks about the importance of looking after widows and orphans, because they were the most isolated, marginalised and poor people in that society – those were people who slipped through the nets. The equivalent in our society includes the kinds of young people we work with – those whom the system has failed, who have fallen through the gaps in society. And if those are the people God is with, then that's where we need to be. If we want to follow Jesus, those are the sorts of places and the sorts of people we will follow him to. If we resist the call to work for justice with the poor of this world, then actually, we are less likely to meet God, because that is where God is.

Our understanding of salvation is not that we have to hang on in this world as long as we can, until God decides he's had enough, and swoops down to exterminate it and carry us off to the new earth and new heaven. Yes, the end times will come, but that is not the be-all and end-all of salvation. Salvation is available now. Not just from outside the world – God is more familiar than that. He gets right in and changes things from the inside out. When Jesus came, he personally experienced darkness, sadness, injustice, destruction, death. When he provided for salvation, it was breaking those things apart from within. So we get in there with the young people – inside the community – we come and make our home here because that is modelling what Jesus did when he came to earth. That is where he started. We want these young people to be saved. We don't equip them to escape this world, we equip them to be able to take this world on and come through.

Niki's diary, 3 February 2006

I haven't read my Bible for about 4 weeks. How naughty is that! It's like my anti new year's resolution! I know it's not actually a good thing to do, but at the same time, I've found it strangely liberating. I've realised that I grew up believing that a Christian is someone who reads their Bible every day and has a quiet time. Actually, although those things are important, they're not the rules by which you judge your life. And more importantly, they're not the rules by which God judges your life. I sincerely sought God last night, and God turned up. He didn't go, 'I'm not going to show up, Niki, because you haven't had enough quiet times recently.' He wanted to be around me, so he came.

I wouldn't say to anyone, 'don't read your Bible', but this is like my personal process of what I have to do to get away from the religion of it because I don't want empty religion. And I don't want to say to other people, 'you have to read your Bible every x amount of time, or you're not a proper Christian,' so really to not be hypocritical, I need to apply it to my own life – to prove to myself that I can miss out on reading the Bible for a while without getting bogged down in a cloud of guilt that then just stops me doing anything properly.

I had a laugh last night. It's exactly nine months since I started at e:merge and I was remembering walking round with Yan on detached, within the first two weeks of being here, and asking him, 'Why don't we pray for people? Why aren't we mentioning God? Why aren't the staff all more outgoing with their faith?' I must have been such a pain. Yan's so brilliant. He would just go, 'Yes, if you want to do that, that's fine.'

Then I remembered how shocked I was when I found out that two of the staff smoked. Honestly!

You'd think it was a cardinal sin. I remember saying to myself, 'What sort of Christians could these be, if they smoke?' I remember thinking, 'What on earth have I come to?!' I think the staff reckon I've changed a lot. I've become a lot more real, a lot more accepting – which is what Jesus was.

I hope I'm not getting cynical with it, though.

Yan

'When they came and told Nathanael that the Messiah had arrived and was from Nazareth, Nathanael said, "Can anything good come from there?"' (John 1:45,46). Jesus was from a place that wasn't rated. Even Bethlehem, where Jesus was born, was at that time considered a minor, unimportant or unattractive place – in Micah it says, 'But you, Bethlehem Ephrathah, though you are small among the clans of Judah . . .' (Micah 5:2). If God lived on earth, I don't think he would live in Henley-on-Thames or Tunbridge Wells. He would care deeply about the people there, of course, and he would want to work with them as partners and welcome them into his life and ministry, but he would live amongst the most downtrodden. If he was on earth today, I think he could have lived here in Bradford. He certainly would have been somewhere rough and poor and looked down upon.

In Exodus, God says to Moses about the Israelites, 'have them make a sanctuary for me, and I will dwell among them' (Exodus 25:8). The tabernacle – God's sanctuary – wasn't on the edge of the settlement. It was in the middle. When people needed God, God said, 'I want to live at the heart of the community.'

After the exclusivity of Moses' individual relationship with God, speaking to him face to face, but alone and on behalf of the rest of the people, God said, 'I want to have a relationship with each and every person' (compare Jeremiah 31:31–34). We strongly believe that God doesn't want to be on the periphery. He wants to be involved and to get his hands dirty.

It means that it's important for us to never do Bradford down. The young people need to know that although the place they live in may not be considered desirable by wider society, it's actually a place God wants to be, a place God esteems. In the same way, we try to make sure that we talk about Bradford in a positive light. Simple things like trying to encourage them to support their local sports teams rather than, say, Manchester United. They're probably never going to go to Manchester United, and certainly not to a Premiership match, but they could go and watch the Bradford Bulls play rugby or something like that. We try and inspire a pride in the place.

I love Bradford. It's not the most attractive city on earth, but Sharon and I have grown to love it. Why? Because we love the people here, and their history, and we love what God wants to do in their lives.

Niki's diary, 21 February 2006

I've decided to do the counselling course. Diarmuid says e:merge will help pay for it for me, as long as I sign a document saying I'll stay with them for eighteen months after getting the qualification. So it'll mean being around here another three years, but for the sake of getting the counselling qualification, that's what I'm going to do.

19

Don't Let Anyone
Look Down On You . . .

Niki's diary, 2 March 2006

We are interviewing for a new youth worker tomorrow, and for the first time we have a panel of young people actually doing some of the interviewing. There are four of them – Jonny, Darren, Shelly and Claire. What happens is, first the candidate is interviewed by the staff panel – Yan, Sharon and one of the directors. Then the young people come in and everyone watches the candidate's presentation together. Then the staff panel leaves and the young people interview the candidate, with no one else present, except Diarmuid sitting at the back of the room just to supervise but not say anything. I'm not going in to any of the interviews, but I'll be there with the young people just beforehand to settle them if they need it, and so they know I'm supporting them.

Sharon and I worked together to find the right young people to be on the panel – those who were closely involved with the project, so understood its ethos and its objectives. We spent time working with them on what their role was, then Diarmuid had quite a few sessions with them where he explained all about job descriptions and person specifications, training them in asking open questions and thinking about what information they were trying to get from the candidates. There's a scoring system whereby the young people's feedback counts for 40 per cent of the overall score and the staff panel's scoring counts for 50 per cent. The other 10 per cent is made up when the candidate we think we want comes to visit for a day – the overall impression of the staff at that point, before the appointment is confirmed.

I'm quite nervous. Not about the young people, because they are really up for it. They understand the importance of getting the right person for the job, and they have been trained really solidly. I think I'm nervous because I know how much we need someone with the right heart. I've become protective of e:merge now and I would hate us to employ someone who sees this as a bog standard job, and who hasn't got that heart for ministry. I definitely think we need someone who sees the difficulties, and if they're a bit scared – that's fine – but they really must have a heart that says, 'I'm going to do this, even if it's hard, because these young people need me.'

Yan

One of the things we've done this year, which Niki has had a large part in, is getting the young people further involved in what we do. We don't want young people just to be on the receiving end. We want them taking part in the planning, leading and decision-making for e:merge.

It has been acknowledged for a long time in the statutory and voluntary sectors that involving your stakeholders is good practice. In fact, for statutory funding, there will generally be a requirement to demonstrate that it happens in your project. At the purely business end, young people are our majority stakeholders. If they do not come to the project, the project does not exist any more. So it would be complete nonsense if we didn't fully consult and involve them in everything.

Much more importantly, however, involving young people is a central part of our overall objective – which is creating chances for young people to improve their lives. Everything we do for young people will be done better and more effectively if they are involved in it. Giving young people responsibility, trust and a valued job to do is all part of helping them grow and flourish. There is also then a strategic effect as we start to tackle the problems of generations-old deprivation by putting the young people themselves at the centre of the solution.

You can start with simple things. When we merged to create the new Friday night congregation, we got the young people themselves to think of a name for it – and they called it Xstream. Then we ran a competition to design the logo and the winner came up with a design like a big cut-out X with a stream of water flowing through it. This was chosen from seven or eight entries. By making it their thing, we immediately created buy-in. The young people have the sense that this is something that they own, rather than something that is being done to them. They engage.

For a long time now we have had a youth council that meets regularly and makes recommendations to the staff team about the way e:merge is run. They are really the body for feeding back the young people's views on the project and how its basic provision can be practically improved. So, for example, we changed the times of the drop-in sessions because of youth council feedback. They said the times were not the best for young people who had other responsibilities, like work or college, so we changed them to have longer sessions, slightly less frequently.

We have had young people leading cell groups for some time. We call them peer leaders. There is masses of research and evidence showing that young people – especially those who are vulnerable – will often open up more quickly to their peers than to adults. It's really exciting when you see young people praying together and talking to each other, and helping to teach each other, without us always telling them what to do. As with the students for the Academy, we're careful who we select for the job, because we want to find the young people for whom this opportunity will really take them on another step – not the ones who are not quite ready for it just yet. We want to set them up to succeed.

Sharon takes the lead in the process. Sometimes the young people express an interest or are very obviously leaders and visible as such. Others we observe and then suggest it to them quietly and gently, to see what they reckon. We take it all slowly, which is part of ensuring they are fully ready, they have the skills to do a good job, and they trust themselves as well as us trusting them. Training will involve discussing cell values; how to talk about what's going on in school or home life, how to deal with issues that the young people raise in their cells, how to ask questions, and some Bible study. Once they've done that, they will be paired with an existing cell leader and will become their assistant leader. This enables them to observe how it's done, and begin to take some of the responsibility gradually. They know that we are there, and they can call on us if they need to. In any case, since most of our young people at Xstream are under eighteen, we are obliged to have an adult present in every room where the young people are meeting together, so there's no sense of sending them off alone to get on with it.

In terms of young people's involvement in recruiting staff, they did have some involvement in Niki's appointment. They were present when she delivered her presentation. However, she wasn't interviewed by them, and the decision was much more weighted towards the directors and staff at that stage. When we recruited for the latest youth worker position, there was a very strong element of the young people having a say in who was offered the job. That is a way to help ensure we do get the right person, because young people know what they need. They know what they are looking for in terms of a person's attitude and ideas, and they are very adept at sussing someone out. I think it also helps in introducing the new staff member to the project. Even with really good induction, the first few weeks can be hard work, as you start to learn the job and face the realities of living and working in an uncomfortable area. When the young people know that they themselves – represented by their peers – have had a hand in the recruitment, it helps create relationship right from the start. I wouldn't say it solves the problem entirely, because it will always take a long time for young people to trust a new person on a deep and individual level, but the foundation is there. The young people are not being presented with someone who the directors or staff think they should have – they are getting someone they have helped choose themselves. They straight away have a stake in making it work for that new person.

Then of course, it's fantastic experience for the young people. It gives them a chance to practice work-related skills in a comfortable environment. They learn skills to do with questioning, using judgement and making decisions. It's not a nod, or lip service. It empowers them, literally, as they have some of the power over who will come to work at e:merge.

If you're going to do that, you have to be prepared to carry it through, though and it can get messy. In fact, for that latest recruitment, it led to a real crunch situation, because the staff panel's scoring and the young people's scoring did not add up to the same conclusion. It took us a bit of time to sort that one out.

Niki's diary, 11 March 2006

The prayer team we have set up for Friday nights is really brilliant. Yan, Sharon, John and I had been saying that when young people want prayer we should have a team of other young people to pray for them. So we set that up, and asked a few young people if they would be willing to pray for others.

This Friday, one of the girls came up to me after Xstream and said she wanted some prayer. So I said, 'Great, of course – Tina will pray for you – is that OK?' They sat down together, and I saw Tina ask her a few questions, and really listen to what she was saying, and then they just prayed together for a few minutes. Afterwards, they were both smiling and looking kind of peaceful and strengthened. Tina kept looking round once or twice while she was praying, to make sure I was still there, but apart from that, they just got on with it. It was great!

I get Abbi to lead the cell group more and more often now because she's really good at it. She started six months or so ago as my co leader. The girls often listen more to her than to me. I'm not sure why. I mean, she definitely has a gift for it, but also I think it's because she's not an adult, not an authority figure. It's funny, even when it's someone like me who they know and relate to – as long as it's someone who's an adult, they are almost programmed to be unable to concentrate. They will start chatting, without even quite realising, and when I say, 'Can you listen please?' they go, 'Oh, sorry Niki – sorry.' And they stop chatting – for about two minutes. Then something will happen and they'll chat again and stop listening to what I'm saying, yet when I tell them again, they put their hands over their mouths, as though they're surprised that they've started talking again – and they go, 'Sorry Niki,' again and stop talking again. It's quite funny but it's infuriating as well!

With Abbi, because she is so completely one of them, they kind of want to make sure she succeeds, they relate to her more closely and probably think, 'wow, she's talking to the whole group – that's really brave' – and they shut up and listen. Also, I suppose it's because everything she says, and the way she says it, is so directly relevant to them, that it connects more immediately.

Yan

There are loads of immediate benefits to young people serving and working with each other in this project, but there's a strategic effect as well, which is potentially the most important. By involving the young people now in a real way, we create the expectation that they can do something – that they are important and can take responsibility and succeed. That is actually a kind of spiritual warfare. We are directly contradicting the voices that for generations have told people that they are hopeless, that they cannot help themselves, that they will always fail. We are setting up new expectations – Godly expectations which say, yes, you can achieve things. Young people, whatever their backgrounds have been, have great resources to minister to each other. They can be transformed, they can succeed. We are breaking the cycle.

The very fact of trusting a young person to do something is significant. Many young people who come to us have lost any sense of being trusted. If no one trusts you, you feel you have very little significance. You start telling yourself, and believing, that you are not capable of doing anything. We have the opportunity of turning that around. So when new young people come to the project, one of the first things they will experience is young people helping themselves and helping each other. This creates a sense of value, a sense of possibility.

The other thing we want to offer is the safety for young people to make mistakes. Yes, we set them up to succeed, supporting them and training them for everything they do, but if there is a point at which they don't do as well as they could have done, it's not the end of the world. Many of our young people have never had a safe place or safe relationships in which they can make mistakes and not be blamed. Mistakes are such a crucial way for us all to learn. I have always worked to create an environment here where we constantly ask ourselves, 'Is this working?' This is a good way of keeping ourselves from becoming complacent, but it also creates a wider expectation that when things are working, that's great, but when things stop working, that's OK too, because we change them, improve them, and move on. It's not a big deal.

We were doing a weekend residential with some of the young people a few years back, and there was an incident that really reinforced for us the value of peer leading. We had organised the accommodation by cell group, to continue that structure of community and support. Sharon and I were in a chalet with a boys' cell, and the peer leader was called Lee. There was a boy in that cell who was experiencing a lot of bullying at school. We'd been in contact with his mother already, and although she'd been into school a number of times, there didn't seem to be any way to deal with it. As a family, they were finding it incredibly hard, and this young lad, Paul, was miserable at school.

Sharon and I were staying in a separate part of the boys' chalet, but the walls were paper thin. As she was going to bed, Sharon heard Paul talking with Lee, his cell leader and another cell member, and he was explaining about the bullying that he was experiencing. Both these other lads were at the same school, but they were older than he was, so not in the same classes, and evidently hadn't known about the bullying before.

It was very interesting to hear the advice that they were giving Paul – it wasn't what we would have offered. Lee, who was the cell leader, said to Paul,

'Don't tell the teachers. Come and find me instead or find one of the older lads that are in the congregation when it happens, and get us to help you deal with it.' He gave some other tips about dealing with it, but his main thrust was, 'Don't tell the teacher because that won't help – tell us and we will help you. We can make sure you are seen with us – and we're bigger and older. You can talk to us about it whenever it happens, and we'll make sure you are not alone in vulnerable places or times.'

Before this, Paul had already tried telling the teachers about the bullying, and it had been making things worse, because the bullies found out that he had told. He became even more of a target and they became sneakier and more sly about how they did it, so it was harder for the teachers to pick up on it, or even to believe Paul when he said what was happening. Now, for the first time, Paul was getting some solid advice and a strategy from other young people who from their own experience knew what was most likely to work. Paul acted on their advice, and the situation improved. I won't say he's never a target for bullies any more, but it has definitely improved – because he got good advice from people that understood his world. Also, the very fact of having that conversation – of opening up himself and then finding he got supportive advice from the other lads – I think made him feel part of the community with the other young people. So he knows he has people sticking up for him, and that in itself makes him seem less alone and a target for bullies.

The cell leader, Lee, and Sharon were cleaning out the room the next day, ready to leave, and Sharon mentioned it to him. She said that she'd heard bits of the conversation, and she told Lee that she thought he'd handled it very well. She did say to him that it wasn't the advice she would have given – but she didn't override it in any way. She said, 'It was great that Paul felt able to talk about that situation, and that you could offer him some strategies.' Young people have a lot of resources for each other to help them cope with situations, because often the situation has happened to another young person before. If you can put young people in sensible structures and create a sense of community and trust, and if you can select some solid peer leaders who you train and support carefully, and show you have confidence in, and then if you stand back and try to avoid meddling and let them get on with it, it is always amazing how much strength and resources start to come out.

Niki's diary, 23 March 2006

Julie showed me this poem she wrote about me in the first few weeks I was getting to know her at e:merge. We were round my house this evening, and discovered we both have poem books where we stick our favourite poems in, and write some ourselves. She was reading some of hers out to me, then she suddenly stopped and said, 'Oh, I can't read this one out to you, Niki.' At first, she looked horrified, but then she started laughing. I asked, 'What's wrong with it?' and she just kept giggling, so I reached over and she gave me the book and I read it.

I don't understand her
What does she want
Why is she here

Why is she so nice
She clearly doesn't belong
She's weird

I wish she would go away
What's the hidden agenda
She'll soon get fed up and leave me alone
I hope

She doesn't even know me
Yet she accepts me
Even though I'm horrible to her
She's still nice to me
It's very annoying
She's geeky and stuck up
She thinks she's Little Miss Perfect
Never does any wrong

She seems to have a lot of faith
She's trying to help me
Well she can stick her faith and kindness
Cos I don't need it
And most certainly don't want it

When I finished, she went quiet and I think she was worried I might be upset, but for me it was brilliant, because it showed me what had been in her mind right back at that time where I was finding everything really hard, too, and feeling like I wasn't getting anywhere. I just sighed, and laughed, and said, 'Now I get it.' She came over and gave me a hug.

Yan

There are these practical and structural ways of listening to young people – but there is also an attitude that I think you need to have, which says, 'I'm going to listen before I talk.'

It's very interesting when you find out what people's expectations and preconceptions are when you first arrive in an area, or are setting up a project. Not just with the young people, but throughout the community, there is a strong presumption that any Christian person or project is coming in to tell everyone else what to do.

If someone is expecting you to think you know best, that you have more answers than they do, they will not be open to what you have to say. If someone sees your life and knows you are a genuine person who still has problems, but has found a way of dealing with them, they will be more likely to relate positively to you. If you actually go out and start by asking them questions, and listening to what they have to say, then you are building a totally different relationship to the one they expect. It's a relationship that says, 'I'm the same as you – we have equal value – my faith does not make me more important, more valued or more intelligent than you. Both of us have things to say and do that will enrich the other person's life.' It isn't one-way traffic. That's what we have tried to do.

At the basic level, we constantly ask young people what they think they need from e:merge – not with a promise to do whatever they want, but with an absolute commitment to take everything they say into account, consider it carefully and act on it in the way we judge to be most appropriate. If you look at Jesus' ministry, he often asked questions and listened to people. For example, in John 5:6 when Jesus healed the man at the pool of Bethesda, it must have been pretty obvious that the man was there because he wanted to be healed – that's what the pool was all about. Yet Jesus' first action, on seeing him, is to ask, 'Do you want to get well?' It's when the man says yes that Jesus moves and heals him.

Something similar happens with the two blind men in Matthew 20:29–34 – they attract Jesus' attention, shouting out for mercy, but even so, when he stops, Jesus asks them, 'What do you want me to do for you?'

I think this demonstrates that Jesus respects people's free will, rather than taking his own agenda and placing it on other people. I think it also shows that there is something incredibly powerful – spiritually powerful – in entering into genuine conversation with someone and they themselves stating what their need is, before the action takes place. If you walk a journey with someone, you talk with them, you don't preach at them.

Niki's diary, 24 March 2006

We've got Derek here this week. He's the guy they interviewed for the youth work job and the young people wanted him, but the staff and directors felt he didn't have enough experience and decided not to appoint anyone to the job. When they spoke to Derek, he just said, 'Let me try it, let me come up and see what it's like.' So Yan, Sharon and Diarmuid agreed for him to do a short term placement here as part of the college course he's finishing.

The young people were fantastic at the interviews – although Jonny only just made it. They saw Derek come in when he first arrived, and he was wearing this amazingly smart suit, really posh tie and big, black, well polished shoes. I have to admit, he looked quite funny – because the rest of him looks like a skater boy. He's got funky black rimmed glasses, his hair is curly and sticking out and he's quite tall and gangly. I suppose he was a bit nervous about the interview, too, so that didn't help. As soon as Jonny caught sight of him, he clutched his mouth and ran out into the other room, where he absolutely fell about laughing, and then of course all the others caught it, too. Utterly helpless. I said, 'Jonny, you can't go and interview the guy unless you stop laughing.' I absolutely forbade him to go in there if he was going to lose it in front of Derek. The others all decided they weren't going to look at Jonny during the interview because they knew he'd make them crack up again. They only just got through it.

As soon as the young people came out of the interview with Derek, they went, 'It's him, Niki – definitely.' It was a really hard one, because although the staff didn't feel strongly enough to appoint, they knew they couldn't deny what the young people were saying either. So we're sort of in limbo about it.

20

For Bradford 4

Niki's diary, 31 March 2006

I do actually feel really optimistic all of a sudden. Since deciding to do the counselling course, and therefore to stay at e:merge longer than this year, I just feel really positive. Loads of things have suddenly slotted into place. I don't know why it is – it's maybe just the security of me knowing I'm going to be here for at least another year, but, well, it's amazing really. I feel positive.

Yesterday I decided that I wasn't praying enough and that I needed to fast. I hate fasting. I usually cave in by teatime, but this time I caved in about one in the morning. I was so hungry I had to have a banana, but I just kept praying.

I wasn't saying very much really, just 'God we need you, I need you, I need to make sense of things', because at the end of the day, God moves in mysterious ways and you're never going to be able to understand completely what he's doing every moment of the day.

The same day, when I was fasting, we got the opportunity to pray for Kirsty. She has never asked for prayer before, so it was like, wow! And normally I'd panic a bit and be like, 'Oh my goodness, what shall I pray? I don't know what to do.' But this time, I felt confident.

I didn't rush through it, I just spent a bit of time. I asked her to open up her heart to God and just give him a chance and I said, 'I'm going to pray for you and if I stop praying, that's your moment to talk to God if you want to,' and she did. We asked God to give her peace and to comfort her and help her in the situation that she was in.

She didn't say anything at the time, and I know she's completely uncertain about whether to believe in God or not, which is fair enough, but she texted me later and said, 'By the way I did feel God.' That was pretty cool.

None of this is easy. It's not sudden answers and immediate miracles. It's up and down but overall, it's going up.

Yan

You can't predict what this kind of job will be like – that's why it's so hard for people to decide whether to come here. You literally don't know what you're letting yourself in for. If someone is thinking about possibly doing this kind of work for the first time, I would definitely recommend that they come and work here for a week – or at a similar project in another city – just to get a feel for it. We have to recruit people who will see the need, and respond to it. They don't have to be a particular type of person, or special in some way, but they do need a big heart for young people and a good measure of perseverance.

We had somebody recently who applied for a job and came and spent a few days with us and she just decided that it wasn't the right thing for her. I respect that – she gave it a go, she was open to the possibility. That's all we can really ask of people.

Niki changed so much over the first year she was with us. By the end of it, she was unrecognisable from the this-is-how-things-are Niki we saw arrive. She is more confident, and has really found her feet. She has started to understand how some of the ways we have traditionally expressed Christianity are not relevant here, but that the love, grace, forgiveness and generosity of God are more relevant than ever. The kids like her – they trust her and value her because they have seen that she lives her life in accordance with the faith she talks about – she is genuine. She will walk with them. I am really glad she is staying with us – I believe she will help us accomplish a lot.

Niki's diary, 4 April 2006

I know that people look at me and think, wow, over this year, she's really changed. Because I have. I'm less easily shocked, I'm not so black and white, I'm more open to seeing every side of a situation – even when that openness challenges my faith. I may even wear more sports gear . . .

I have found ways of communicating with these kids that I never had before but these are all the obvious things, the outside things. It's as though I've changed the frame without changing the painting. My faith hasn't changed, but the way I express it, the way I communicate it, the expectations I put with it, they've changed massively.

I went home to see my mum at the weekend, and she said, 'Niki, you're just the same. You are relating to different people in a different environment to before, but you are the same person.' That was really encouraging, because she knows. And actually, the way people initially see me is a lot to do with their own perceptions and prejudices. I look like a nice girl – a soft, blond, sweet girl. I realise that. And to some people that means I look like someone from a sheltered background who is naïve about the world. Someone I worked with a few years back, when I told him about the kids in Bradford, said to me, 'I can't imagine _you_ getting involved with those kinds of people,' and I was mad, absolutely furious with him. He saw my comfortable, comparatively well off background, my respectable parents, and completely missed my heart.

My heart hasn't changed. What I have always, always wanted is a relevant faith. That's still the same. If anything, it's stronger. Not in the sense that I'm always happy and chirpy – far from it. But in the sense that I'm convinced of how much work there is to be done, and that I can be part of it, and that Jesus is the answer.

I'm no one extraordinary. I mean, lots of people have those kinds of feelings – to want to do something real for God. The thing is, what do you do with that feeling? A lot of people in a lot of churches do an enormous amount of work for the poor, and for deprived communities, like the people back home in my old church – a very mainstream sort of church. Some of them give money, some of them pray and I need them to do that – I really rely on them, actually, probably

more than they realise. But then a few of them,
like me, will say, 'Enough. I'm going to get up
and go there. I'm going to take a risk and live in
the community and work with them' and I think,
whatever is speaking in your heart, that's what
God requires of you, whatever that is. It's having
the courage to examine your heart and face the
consequences.

When I arrived here I know I was perceived as
being the kind of happy Christian who thinks
that loving God is all about waving your arms
about and not dropping litter. During the last 12
months, I think I have become more relevant and
less judgemental. I have understood more about
who God is in communities like Bradford 4 – his
forgiveness, his persistence, his love. However,
because of the sense of isolation here, and the lack
of understanding from some sectors of the church
family, I have also risked becoming cynical and
critical. I want to keep the good things I've learnt,
but I want to retain that spiritual optimism, too.
Yes, I am a happy clappy Christian. And I'm
incredibly fortunate to have the background I
have – a stable environment with capable parents
who taught me about Jesus and love me no matter
what. I can't deny that background, and why
would I want to? I want to believe in the impossible,
have faith in the faithless and I want to serve a
massive God.

Yan

These are the things that I think we do well at e:merge:
we walk the walk with young people for as long as

they need us. We don't start with our own agenda. We start with the agenda of the person in need. We combine bringing the possibility of faith with real, concrete attention to the needs, here and now, of the young people. We will do whatever it takes to make things work for each individual we come into contact with. We are prepared to stick it out – we don't look for short-term results. We actually, genuinely care. We want young people to succeed. We see worship and church and prayer as a combination of everything we do in life – particularly what we do for others – rather than something that happens in an hour on a Sunday morning and two on a Tuesday evening. In all these things, what we try and do is understand who Jesus is in this community, and then try to be like him. The Jesus of the Bible. The unusual, passionate, compassionate, committed, generous, patient, loving, challenging, hard-working, intimate, uncompromising, non-judgemental, welcoming Jesus.

Niki's diary, 12 April 2006

Derek started for real this week as our new youth worker. He is so the right choice! As soon as he arrived for his placement, we all thought he was great, and actually, by the end of the first week, everyone realised that he very obviously is the one! Diarmuid had a chat with him part way through and said, 'The position is still open, so if it works for you and it works for us, it's yours.'

He is fun, and has a good heart and is very humble as well as lively and quietly confident. The kids think he's great. With his fuzzy hair and glasses, they decided he looks a bit like a computer expert, so as soon as he arrived and I introduced him to a few of the young people at drop in, they were calling him a geek. One lad who was trying to be a bit clever and aggressive went up to him, and just to his face said, 'You're a big geek.' So Derek went, 'Yes I am. And proud of it,' and the lad just did not know what to do. He was nonplussed for a second, and the other kids there just laughed, and then the lad went, 'Yeah, cool. Nice one, geek,' and they all think Derek is brilliant now!

Derek and I have decided to do a bit of a display thing for Easter, and we're inviting some of the young people to come and be shown round it and then we'll take them to McDonalds afterwards. We're just putting little things like stations of the cross around the building. Some nails. A crown made of thorny twigs. A robe. I'm writing a small explanation of each one – what it means and what part it played in the Easter story. Then we'll show the young people round and answer any questions they have. I'm looking forward to it. I really want to say to the young people that this is for you, you know. He did it for you.

Yan

I think the hope of God lies in this: that no matter what our young people have been through, they can come through it and out onto the other side. Since I have been here, I have really learnt to admire the human spirit and our capacity to overcome pain. You listen to some of the young people's stories, and see what has happened in their lives, and you stand back in awe really at God's creation. God created us so that a fire of creativity, love and faith burned somewhere inside us and even the worst experiences in the world wouldn't completely extinguish it. God is so gracious, and so generous. When you think what people do to each other in this world. God still says, 'Yes, I want to give you freedom.'

Just as in the Old Testament, God decided to come and dwell by his tabernacle in the centre of his people's community, so in the New Testament Jesus came in person to bring us salvation and freedom. And now, he gives us the Holy Spirit to be present with us. We do not pray to a God who is far away. The nature of God is that he is with us – with us through everything – not just when we succeed or make the right choices. God is not interested in counting the things we get wrong. He is interested in leaving those things behind, us learning from them and then moving on. Christ didn't die when we started repenting. He died when we were still in sin (see Romans 5:8). His name is Immanuel – God with us – God right here. God didn't shout, 'Come out of your mess, I'm saving you!' He got into the mess with us and then showed us the way out of it.

Niki's diary, 16 April 2006

It's a year since I came to e:merge. I never thought I'd feel so right here, so at home. I only realised this in the last few weeks, but it's part of belonging. We talk about belong, believe, behave for our youth congregation. Well, it's actually the same for me – once I felt like I belonged to e:merge, was a genuine and important part of it, that's when I started to flourish and express myself, and really believe in what we do here and the way we do it. It takes time.

It's not like everything's wonderful, because it's clearly not, but the thing is, I think you feel fulfilled and happier when you're doing what you know you should be doing, when you know you're in the right place, when you've got that confidence, and other people believe in you. I suppose it's taken me a year to get to the place where I feel all those things. I feel confident in my position and affirmed by other members of staff, so I can take control of things a bit more. I have established friendships of trust with the young people, so I feel less alone.

The main thing is, these young women and men still need Jesus, and they still need me. In a way, I need them, too. There's work to do and I'm here to do it. It's only just begun, really.

21

Are You Called?

Yan

People often think you need a specific calling to do this kind of work. They think you need something special to work here – like, this is not the norm, you stay in your world until God very specifically calls you out and kind of hand-picks you to come here. I think that's rubbish. I happen to think that the people who work here are really amazing, and special, and that yes, definitely, God has called them to be here – and I'm really grateful for that, because I need them around me. But when I look at our website, and the pictures on the staff page, I can't help thinking that we're a very normal, not particularly good-looking ragbag of assorted people. We are special, but only in the same way as anyone else is special. If there's anything we have that marks us out, I think it's that we are genuine. Each of us is true to who and what we are.

Are we called? It's a funny question. Yes of course we're called – everyone is called to work with the poor and marginalised because that's what God is all about. I don't think there's anything intrinsically different about us here that makes us called. I think, maybe, God is constantly calling out for people to come and fight these kinds of battles with him, and a few of us hear him, and an even fewer say, 'OK, God, send me.' And the people who say that – well, they end up being the ones who were called. I think it's very possible that a lot more people are called than are actually here.

The reason that Sharon and I are here, the reason why others who work here stay, is that if we don't stand up for these people, who will? If someone doesn't speak up for the young people, they haven't got a chance. They haven't got a voice, have they? They've no chance of saying why the system's failed them, why their parents have failed them, why things are just a mess and at the end of the day, they don't really care who has failed, they just need a way out. So I just think they haven't got a voice and if somebody doesn't speak up for them, then no one will.

Sharon

Yes, I was called here – but also, it was my choice. I think it's possible that I could have served God in a very different way with my life. Before coming here I was an English teacher and loved it. I could have done that happily for years. However, God definitely interrupted that course in my life by directing my attention towards youth work and ultimately Bradford. And in much the same way, after we'd been here for four years, I can remember God interrupting my understanding of our role, which I had seen as relatively short term, by asking us, 'So, are you going to opt in and be here in the way that young people here have to opt in, because they don't have a choice? Or are you going to continue believing that if it all goes wrong, if you get fed up with it and don't like it anymore, you can always opt out and go "home"? That's not an option they have. This is their only "home". So what are you going to do – commit and make this your long-term home, too, or hold on to your escape clause?'

We are very blessed that as well as falling in love with each other, Yan and I were compatible in terms of the kind of ministry we knew God was calling us to. Not every couple has the experience of living, working and learning together in the way that we do – and not everyone would want to. Choosing to have our lives so integrated makes things simple in one sense, but sometimes it's exhaustingly intense. We get to share all the ups and downs, like the heart-breaking moments when someone leaves and then the elation when it goes right for a young person we care about. But, without hesitation, I can say that I'm glad God drew us here together and I wouldn't have it any other way.

John

There's no shining light that brought me to e:merge. I don't think I received any special revelation from God that I was to move to this particular area of Bradford or work with these particular young people – certainly nothing audible. But I had read the Bible.

I did a summer football camp – as a volunteer. Then Yan asked me to stay. I don't know what made me decide to give it a go. I didn't even know whether youth work was going to be my main thing. The day I moved in to the flat, two young guys who went to drop-ins at the project helped me move in. I was really chuffed. I thought, wow, these kids are kind and helpful, and want to make me welcome. When they'd gone I discovered they'd stolen a load of my footballs.

I wonder if most people really understand what the call to follow Christ is about. As much as he sends out a call, I think God also just asks a question – 'Who will go?' – and anyone *could* respond, but not everyone does. There needs to be a call to action that goes beyond our very comfortable church environments. We're not talking about going slightly outside our comfort zone. We're talking about a complete sacrificial lifestyle. Could you give up everything for Christ? Everything? Could you go anywhere for him? Could you die for him? Because there are much worse places than Bradford to go to, where people need God.

My problem is, I stand in church and people all around me are singing, 'Jesus, I would go to the ends of the earth,' and they're swaying back and forth with their eyes closed and their hands all over the place and massive, earnest expressions on their faces, and for some reason I can't sing it. Because honestly, I don't know if I could. Could I go anywhere God asked me to – anywhere? Could I live every second of my life as an act of worship? Could I treat everything I have, from money to possessions to relationships, as if I've just borrowed them from God? Could I, if he really demanded it of me, give everything up for Jesus? I want to. I want to be able to. But I can't sing those songs with my hand totally on my heart – I doubt myself.

If I were Abraham could I sacrifice Isaac – just because God asked me to? Sometimes I look into my baby daughter's eyes and wonder – do I really love Jesus more than I love you? I want to know for sure, if it came to the crunch – would Jesus come out on top? So when we sing those songs, I wonder, 'Is it me? Is there something I don't get or am I reading a different

Bible?' Because in my Bible it doesn't say, 'if you feel like it, stand up for the oppressed', or 'when you've got surplus money, give to the poor'. What are we really singing?

I believe that justice is high on God's agenda and I believe that I must do my bit as part of the church to bring that justice about. Whether that is on a global scale or a personal one. So I don't think God gave me a specific calling to this place or these people, because I don't think he needed to. It's written in black and white throughout 66 books.

Once you're here, whatever other reasons you've come for, you do it for the young people. A lot of these young people are hard. They have had hard lives already, even at a young age, and they are hardened because of that. They're not sweet or cuddly or immediately rewarding. But if you're patient, and they see you're genuine, and in time if you get to know them, they're absolutely fantastic, they really are. They're difficult. They're hard work. They don't behave the way they should, or even in ways you could predict and things aren't black and white with them. You have to roll with the punches a bit, and yet, there's something about people who have known hardship so early on in life. I like being with them. They're frustrating, but also, they have got so creative, so imaginative in the way they take on the world. At the end of the day, they're my favourites, I can't help it.

So that's where my calling is – with the kids – and I don't think you need a specific calling to work here. I think God has called you already. I've had times when I've been telling young people here about Jesus, how there's a God who loves us and wants to forgive us, and they just say, 'If this is as important as you say, why hasn't someone told me before?' That really hits you. Why should you feel you have to get a 'special touch' in order to come and walk with needy young people, or to tell them that God loves them and is interested in changing their lives?

Niki

I think you need a specific calling to work somewhere like this. It's not for everybody, and it's not the kind of thing someone can just turn up and say, oh yes, I think I should probably do a bit of this for a while. I've always known that I've been called to do something rock hard. I just knew. I don't think you have to be an extraordinary person, but you need a heart that says, 'whatever it takes – that's what I'll have to give.'

I'm not anyone extraordinary, but I do have a deep desire to do what God wants me to do in life. I suppose I have a sort of fear because I know that if I don't do what God is calling me to, then I'll miss out in some way. Not that God's call is always easy, but it is the only way to have the most significant life you can have, and I always want to walk in that calling. So to me, if God says, 'Go and live in a mud hut in Africa,' I'd have to do it, regardless of whether I wanted to or not, and that's why I came here.

The interesting thing here though is that at the start, I didn't feel God specifically say, 'Niki – do this thing. Go to Bradford.' It was much scarier because it was more like my decision. What has happened is that as I've done it, he's called me to it from inside it. I naturally started working with the girls, and building friendships and then going towards the counselling route, and as that's happened, it has brought back things from earlier in my life – the sense that actually,

I've always wanted to work with young women from troubled backgrounds. As I've gone along, God has confirmed more and more that this is where I'm to be. Who knows for how long – you can never say. But for now, this is where I am, and as long as I'm here, I want to serve wholeheartedly.

Derek

I actually found the job advert a little intimidating. It started by asking, 'Do you have the courage to have faith in the faithless,' and then it said '90 per cent of people won't cut it at e:merge'! I thought the job looked cool, though, so after a bit of deliberation I sent in an application. I just said to God – I don't think I'm in the 10 per cent, Lord, but it's really up to you.

I was coming to the end of studying for a national youth work qualification, and I'd been thinking for a while about what my next step should be, but without much revelation. Also, I had been a bit apathetic in applying for jobs because I was scared of the disappointment and rejection I would feel if I didn't get them. When e:merge invited me for interview, I said to God, 'Right. I'm going to go for this with the sort of enthusiasm and commitment that will mean if I don't get it I'll be really gutted. I'm going to risk it.'

The interview seemed to go well. A couple of answers I could have given better, but on the whole it was OK. Diarmuid was relaxed and very reassuring, and the young people were amazing. At first I was just impressed at the power entrusted to them by the staff, but then as they interviewed me, I was astounded at the way they carried it off. They completely justified the power they had been given.

Then Diarmuid rang me and said they'd decided not to appoint anyone. It was really weird. With other job applications and interviews, I'd felt a massive peace about being told I wasn't the right candidate, but when Diarmuid rang, I just felt confused about what God wanted.

I chatted with my college tutor about it, and he suggested I ask if I could spend some time with e:merge on a voluntary basis, which would show them I was up to the job. I thought this was a really arrogant thing to do, but I needed to do a placement for my college course anyway so I plucked up the courage to ring Diarmuid and said how impressed I'd been with e:merge, and was there any chance I could come and spend a few weeks with them on a voluntary basis. He said yes.

Diarmuid told me they were still looking for someone for the permanent job, and that if the placement went well I would have a chance. Almost the moment I started my placement I desperately wanted the job. Things at e:merge just seemed to be done right. Everything was a really cool balance of quality work, freedom to get on and do stuff with young people, and good systems in place to ensure everything was done well, without the policies and practices being at all restrictive or time consuming. As well as that, the young people I was starting to meet were brilliant, and the more I got to know the team as well, the more I wanted to be a part of it. At the end of the placement, they told me they wanted me to stay.

I don't think at any point God specifically said, 'Derek this is where I want you to go,' but I do really believe that as the process went on, God was gradually revealing that that's what he wanted for my wife and me. The move to Bradford was better for her with getting to work, and working at e:merge has been perfect for me. I feel like God does that – shows you a little bit at a time, gets you ready for the bigger picture. The more I look at how it all panned out, the more it all adds up as too many coincidences to be just chance.

I also think a large part of God's calling for us is the desires he has put in our hearts. I do feel God called me to work with young people, because I don't think he'd have put that desire in me otherwise. My heart tells me to get alongside these young people, spend time getting to know them and help them if and when I can. I think if you can't say that then this kind of work wouldn't be right for you.

There are lots of things I want to do or achieve in life, both personally and professionally. One day I think I'd like to be involved in building the world's biggest skateboarding park!! For now though, I'm just taking each day as it comes, enjoying spending it with God, my wife and e:merge, and taking every opportunity I can to be everything God wants me to be. I'm not always great at it, but I think he knows I'm trying.

22

In Our Own Words:
Students at the Academy

Darren

I have been coming to e:merge for about 8 years. Before I came, my brother and sister came here. Now I'm on the Academy. It's done loads for me, but one of the biggest things is that I had met some wrong people and coming to e:merge helps me stay away from them. I didn't really want to learn at school, but at the Academy it's different. It's to do with your mind – it's explaining things so you can understand them and then make your own decisions, work out things for yourself. I have known the leaders since I was young. John has really been my role model. Now I'm doing some PE teaching at the local school, which will hopefully get me a job by the end if I do OK.

Al

The first day I came here, I thought it's going to be a waste of time and I'll learn nothing but I guess I was wrong. I have learnt lots of things by being here. I also thought it's going to be boring with only writing work, well, it's not only writing it's also practical which I like. Before I came here, I thought I knew everything about sports but I was just kidding myself. After a few weeks coming to e:merge, I knew most of things about sports. Also by coming to e:merge you will know about yourself better, I'm 100 per cent certain now that I am going to achieve something in life by coming to e:merge.

e:merge has really friendly people, and every member of staff is supportive. The Academy students are also friendly – the first day I came here I thought I was not going to get along with the Academy well but now I get along with everyone well.

Ray

In my eight weeks here at e:merge I believe I have improved immensely. I have improved my fitness dramatically although I am still behind some others. My confidence is always high now despite the first six weeks being quite hard for me but the last two weeks I have started believing in myself a lot more because I know now I have the potential to become a really good coach.

My first six weeks were hard for me because I felt like I wasn't worthy enough to be here because I was behind everybody in fitness and my personality wasn't really showing but over the last two weeks I feel more comfortable and I am putting more effort into sessions as I was not doing my best and not showing my strengths.

Samina

My family consists of my mum and stepdad and my dad and stepmum. My stepmum has three daughters and a son. I also have two half-sisters by my dad's first marriage. Both my dad and stepmum are alcoholics struggling to recover. None of these members of my family have any faith, and alcohol is a recurring problem.

After my parents' divorce, I felt I had the freedom to explore things more and when a friend brought me to Xstream I became intrigued by faith for the first time. Almost a month ago, I was baptised and after growing up through alcoholism, divorce and a sudden conversion to a foreign culture, I can proudly proclaim myself a Christian. Why do I follow Jesus? Because I have never known people who give off such warmth and make me feel so complete and so loved. I have never before known happiness like this and now I have found it I intend to hold on to it.

Patrick

From the first moment I got here I was nervous as I didn't know what the people would be like. My first impression when I saw them: I thought they were going to be cocky because they were just chatting about themselves. But as I got to know them I realised that they were all very cool and ever since day one we have come together as a group and we are getting on like a house on fire! The staff are friendly and I get on really well with them all!

The reason I joined the Academy is because I wanted to get sports qualifications, especially cricket as that is the sport I most enjoy, but the main reason is to get a job at the end of it and I would like to go further into youth work as that is what I would like to do.

I think I have improved a lot especially with my physical fitness and my motivation and encouragement to all my other team mates and have improved my communication towards others as well as my leadership skills.

Tom

At the beginning when I was at school I got thrown out. I was lost and never knew where to go. I got involved in the wrong crowds but I do take all the blame because I made my own decisions (which were wrong). I really started hating my life every day; when I woke up I just hated. My family never supported me in any way – I was just lost and never knew what to do, I was going to be left dead or in prison. One day I heard about a place called e:merge.

When I first heard about e:merge, I thought it was going to be a waste of time. But anything was better than the way I used to live so I decided to give it a go. However, now that I have been here for seven weeks I enjoy every day that I am here. The reasons I enjoy coming here is because every day is different from the day that has past. The main reason I love coming here is because the staff here are just the best. Jenny and John – you can't ask for better teachers than them two. I would also like to say that the Academy pupils are excellent. I would not pick anyone else to spend a year with.

Every single day we learn something new, not a day will go past that the staff at e:merge will teach us something that we already know. I would tell you about the bad things about e:merge but honestly I can't think of one. It has been welcoming. The boss here is a great laugh. I really enjoy doing youth work and sports leadership. My journey overall at e:merge has been just the best. I also learnt here that darts is not a sport.

I would recommend e:merge to anyone. I got a second chance and I have leapt for it. I just thank all the people at e:merge for just being what they are and for giving me a second chance.

23

An Ending

Niki's diary, 7 June 2006

Julie's uncle has moved out!!! I can't believe it.
He got into a relationship with some woman, and
just went, over the weekend. Julie came in and told
me, and honestly, she looked about three years
younger with all the relief and joy. It's amazing.
After all this time, and all our prayer. No more
beatings, no more putting up with it. It's over! Oh
God, thank you, thank you so, so much.

For more information about the work of **e:merge** check out our website at www.emergeonline.org.uk

If you would like to receive our newsletter, make a donation or get some more info then please complete the 'contact us' section on the website, and we will be in touch!

TONY ANTHONY

WITH ANGELA LITTLE

TAMING THE

TIGER

FROM THE DEPTHS OF HELL TO THE
HEIGHTS OF GLORY

The remarkable true story of a Kung Fu
World Champion

978-1-86024-481-0

Foreword by J.John

ONCE AN ADDICT

The fascinating true story of one man's escape from the murky drugs underworld

Barry Woodward

with Andrew Chamberlain

978-1-86024-602-9

KIM GOH

WITH ANDREW CHAMBERLAIN

CONQUERING THE *Dragon*

The true life story of a former triad gang member

978-1-86024-616-6

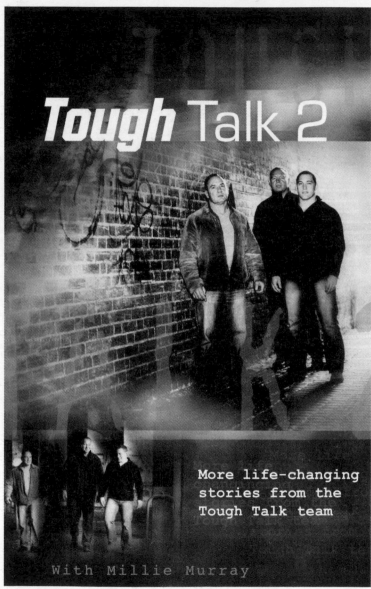

Tough Talk 2

More life-changing
stories from the
Tough Talk team

With Millie Murray

978-1-86024-700-2